T0369048

# GROTON
## Historical Bits and Pieces

James L. Streeter

iUniverse, Inc.
New York Bloomington

*iUniverse books may be ordered through booksellers or by contacting:*

*iUniverse*
*1663 Liberty Drive*
*Bloomington, IN 47403*
*www.iuniverse.com*
*1-800-Authors (1-800-288-4677)*

*Because of the dynamic nature of the Internet, any Web addresses or links contained in this book may have changed since publication and may no longer be valid. The views expressed in this work are solely those of the author and do not necessarily reflect the views of the publisher, and the publisher hereby disclaims any responsibility for them.*

*ISBN: 978-1-4401-7907-5 (sc)*
*ISBN: 978-1-4401-7908-2 (ebook)*

*Printed in the United States of America*

*iUniverse rev. date: 11/20/2009*

# Dedication

The Town of Groton is so fortunate to have Carol W. Kimball as its official town historian. She is extremely knowledgeable and versed on not only the history of Groton but its surrounding communities. Carol is the author of several books, including *The Groton Story*, *The History of Groton in Words & Pictures*, *The Poquonnock Bridge Story*, *Historic Glimpses—Recollections of Days Past in the Mystic River Valley*, *Tales From East of the Thames*, and two *Images of America* books— *Groton* and *Groton Revisited*. She has written a weekly column in the *Day* newspaper since 1985, and several of her articles have appeared in various periodicals, including *Yankee Magazine*, the *Log of Mystic Seaport*, and *Tidings*.

Carol's tireless efforts and dedication to document and report local history places her among the elite of area historians, including Charles R. Stark, Frances Manwaring Caulkins, Mary Virginia Goodman, and Eva Butler. She has been my mentor of sorts and has provided me with the inspiration to continue to document Groton's history.

Our community owes a debt of gratitude to Carol W. Kimball, and dedicating this book to her is a small way of saying "Thank You."

"The history of Groton, whether it be written, verbal, or in graphic form, does not belong to any one individual ... it belongs to, and must be shared with, everyone."

The Author

# Contents

# Acknowledgments

The author would like thank the following people and organizations for contributing information and photographs for the articles written for the *Groton Times* newspaper and in making this book possible: Carol Kimball, Marilyn Comrie, Bill Scarano, Everest Brustolon, Tom Migliaccio, Sal Giordano, Barbara Tarbox, John Santacroce, Marty Artale, Mystic River Historical Society, Robert Bankel, United States Submarine Base New London (Groton), the Chester family, the *Day*, Carol Baker, Bill Hart, John Scott, the Town of Groton, the National Archives, Margaret O'Connell, Janet Lester Crossman, the Groton Ambulance Association, the Hoxie Fire Department, Ken Barton, Roadell Hickman, Don Byles, the Colonial Ledyard Cemetery Association, Hali Keeler, the Bill Memorial Library, Winifred Newbury, the Johnson family, Dorothy Chrissos, Arthur Greenleaf, Virginia Robarge, Shirley (Rabitaille) Viveiros, Mariellen French, "Doc" Patton, the City of Groton, Ann and Alan Bentz, Bob Irons, Sandra Weekes, Alice and Edward Vross, the Strickland family, the Connecticut Department of Transportation, Tony Levesque, the University of Connecticut (Avery Point), Bill Sanford, Bob Sharpe, Ed Stebbins, Robert Welt, Jack Eckert, Robert Austin-LaFrance, and Mark Russell.

I would like to extend a special thank-you to my friend and lighthouse enthusiast Ron Foster, who, through his ingenuity and publishing skills, produced the cover of this book.

The most important acknowledgment goes to my wife, Irma. Throughout the years she has unselfishly sacrificed most of the storage space in our home, which has permitted me to accumulate and stockpile voluminous historical materials (which she calls "Stuff") about Groton. She has also been a "home editor" of sorts, correcting my typos, spelling, and grammatical errors, and providing constructive criticism when it was necessary. Every author should be blessed to have someone like her.

# Foreword

Jim Streeter began writing a weekly column for the *Groton Times* newspaper in September 2004. At first it was just a short article about Groton's past entitled "Didja Know?"—little more than a photograph with a small write-up. In June 2007, the articles were expanded into full-fledged, well-illustrated columns renamed "History Revisited." Jim has gathered a number of these writings into book form, passing along little-known and interesting facts about Groton, Connecticut, which is also known as the "Submarine Capital of the World."

Jim, a Groton native, has always had a liking for the town—past, present, and future. He just finished serving his second term on the Groton Town Council and is presently a councilor in the City of Groton, where he previously served as the deputy mayor.

With the help of others, he was instrumental in the saving, restoration, and relighting of Groton's Avery Point Lighthouse and in establishing the Groton Historical Society. He was a member of Town of Groton's Tercentennial Celebration Committee and the City of Groton's Centennial Committee. Jim's collection of Groton photographs, postcards, and memorabilia is second to none, and through his diligent research, he has gathered a myriad of facts to accompany them. Do you know about "Duffy," the Coast Guard mascot buried at Avery Point, or the Groton Cigar Factory, which once stood at 181 Thames Street? Jim can tell you. He has scoured back issues of newspapers as well as his personal collection to obtain his facts, and he has supplemented them with information gained from informal historical breakfast sessions with fellow history buffs.

Groton has a rich and varied history, and Jim has investigated it, turning up many titillating facts. I was surprised to learn that fumes from the C. M. Shea Fertilizer Company almost closed the Sub Base in 1916, and I knew little about the Quinnipiac Fertilizer Company, established on Pine Island in 1877, a prosperous business purchased and extinguished by Morton Plant in 1903 to purify the sacred air at Branford House and the Griswold Hotel. His columns cover these and a multitude of other subjects, well-researched and often quite astonishing.

It's Jim's belief that Groton's history belongs to the people, and he has produced a readable book that makes it easy to acquire this knowledge. Since Jim is also a crack photographer, the plentiful images reproduced in the book add to its attraction. It's a great addition to our local history bookshelf.

Carol W. Kimball
Groton Town Historian

# Introduction

The town of Groton, Connecticut, is rich in history. Although the official establishment or incorporation of Groton did not occur until May of 1705, its beginnings can be traced back to the early 1640s, and much has been written about the town's early history. Indeed, many find the early history to be important and interesting; however, there has been a lack of recording of what can be considered "modern history."

Just what fits the definition of "modern history" is open to discussion and interesting debate. In my own personal, and possibly liberal sense, it could and should include anything dating from the late 1800s through the 1960s. I stand by the definition listed in the *Merriam-Webster Dictionary*—"a branch of knowledge that records and explains past events."

As a "historic barometer" of sorts, if you are over the age of fifty, the next time you sit with old friends or family members and reminisce about years gone by, you'll probably end up talking about a person, place, or thing that no longer exists but is still in your memory. Yes, to me that can fit the definition of modern history and needs to be documented. One hundred years from now, those people, places, and things from the 1960s will be an important part of our town's history, and to have had it documented will be appreciated.

In September of 2004, I was asked by a staff member of the *Groton Times* newspaper if I would be interested in contributing a short Groton historical piece for publication in their paper. Without hesitation I agreed to do so; however, I took the editorial privilege of writing articles involving "modern history." At first the articles, captioned "Didja Know," were very short, usually one or two short paragraphs with an accompanying photograph. As readers' interest in the articles grew, so did their length. They became full-length features under a section titled "History Revisited."

Unfortunately, distribution of the *Groton Times* paper was limited, and many Groton residents were not in receipt of these historical pieces. My writing of the articles and the limited distribution of the publication was the impetus for creating this book.

This book does not contain every article published in the *Times* but is a selection of those, both large and small, that I felt would be of interest to a large spectrum of readers. So as not to change the contents of the articles, the dates when the articles were published in the *Groton Times* appear in parenthesis at the end of each article. Many of the articles published in this book are accompanied by associated photographs, and appropriate credits for those photos appear in parenthesis at the end of each photo caption.

It is hoped that many will enjoy these articles, and, if interest is great, a second book, containing additional published articles, may also be produced in the future.

The author has all intents of continuing his efforts of documenting the "modern history" of the town of Groton. Anyone who may possess information or photographs relating to a person, place, or thing that is historical in nature to Groton which might be of interest for publication is encouraged to contact the author.

# Chapter 1

## Our Town

# Two Grotons—One Community

Newcomers and visitors arriving in Groton often become confused when they hear the names Town of Groton and City of Groton. Immediately the question arises: "Are there two Grotons?" There is no simple answer to the question, and to understand why the two exist, one must be provided with a short history lesson about Groton.

Groton's beginning can be traced to 1646 when John Winthrop, Jr., the son of the [then] governor of Massachusetts, settled on the Thames River and established a plantation called New London. This settlement extended to both sides of the river and stretched six miles northward from Fishers Island / Long Island Sound.

As early as the 1670s, fishing and coastal vessels were being built in the village on the east bank of the Thames River. The primary means of travel for those wishing to go from one side to the other of the river was by ferryboat. The first ferry landing in Groton was built on the east bank of the river. The shipbuilding trades, in combination with the accessibility to the ferryboat, caused neighborhoods of people and small businesses to spring up along the eastern shore. This area was referred to as "The Bank."

From the beginning, and continuing for over fifty-eight years, residents of the east side of the river pursued their independence from New London. In 1704, the residents on the west side of the river agreed that the inhabitants on the east side should form their own town. In 1705, the Connecticut General Assembly approved and granted a charter to the lands on the east side of the Thames River to become a distinct township, to be called Groton.

As the various [settled] areas of the town grew, they demanded special services. Ultimately, a number of geographical districts, commonly referred to as "fire districts," were established to provide these services. Although the fire districts fall under the purview of the Town of Groton's government, several of them established their own internal governmental structures.

In 1900, the Eastern Shipbuilding Company located in the Groton "Bank" area and began building two mammoth steamships. This created a tremendous boom to the local economy and a dramatic increase in the eastern shoreline's population.

The rapid expansion of shipbuilding and the development of a large summer resort hotel (the Griswold) on the eastern shore of the Thames led several business and civic leaders to become progressive in their thoughts. They felt if they were going to bring the community forward into the modern age they would have to provide the residents with the same privileges and services that the residents of New London were receiving, including water, electricity, and fire and police protection. In an effort to accomplish this, the leaders developed plans to purchase the privately owned Groton Electric Lighting Company. The profits from this company would help defray the cost of providing the desired services.

In December 1900, a petition was submitted to the General Assembly of Connecticut seeking to incorporate the "Bank" and eastern shore area of the Thames River as a "borough" of Groton.

In May of 1903, the Legislature granted approval, and the Borough of Groton was incorporated as a new political subdivision (district) of the Town of Groton. Boundaries, encompassing approximately seven and one half square miles on the Thames River's east shore, were established for the Borough, which accounted for approximately 16 percent of the Town of Groton's forty-five square miles. Originally the Borough was governed by a warden and burgesses system of government.

At the time of incorporation, contingencies were established requiring the residents of the Borough to pay the same amount of taxes to the Town of Groton that other residents of the town paid; however, the Borough would receive, from the Town, reimbursement for the costs of maintaining highways within the Borough and one half of the expenses for operating its own police department, excluding its chief. Borough residents would also contribute a separate tax to the Borough to pay for special services they desired including fire and police protection, a recreational department, trash removal and sewers. A stated amount of profits realized by the Utilities Department were provided to the Borough to offset the cost of these services.

For over sixty-plus years, development within the Borough continued in leaps and bounds. Industries such as Electric Boat Corporation and Pfizer, Inc., established themselves in the Borough and brought thousands of families to the area. Development of the

U.S. Submarine Base and the Coast Guard Training Station also brought many new residents to the area. The economy flourished and the Borough became the "economic jewel" of the town.

In 1964, the Borough of Groton became the City of Groton and was governed by a mayor and council.

The 2000 population census reflects there were just under 40,000 residents in the Town of Groton, with a little over 10,000 living in the City. With the Electric Boat Corporation and Pfizer, Inc., on its tax rolls, the City of Groton continues to be the "economic jewel" for the Town of Groton, contributing approximately 28 percent of the tax base for the Town of Groton.

From time to time, internal government disagreements arise between the Town and City. Although questions and suggestions about consolidation and separation of the Town and City are often the center of discussion, no formal action has ever been pursued.

So to answer the question "Are There Two Grotons?" one must say yes—a "parent," the Town of Groton, and its "offspring," the City of Groton, both coexisting in the same "residence." *(August 29, 2008)*

# Groton Town Seal

Prior to 1935, the Town of Groton had no design for an official seal. The State of Connecticut was about to celebrate its three hundredth anniversary, and Groton's Committee for the Connecticut Tercentenary arranged to have a seal designed to use on its stationery and publications for the tercentennial celebration. Theodore Norton of Mystic, who was the Advisory Secretary for the Tercentenary Central Committee, subsequently designed a seal.

The seal was in the shape of a triangle to symbolize the fact that it was designed in honor of the Connecticut Tercentenary—one side for each hundred years in the state's history. Inside the triangle were three different drawings representing the three most prominent maritime activities in Groton's three largest villages' history—a drawing of a boat hull from a model of a clipper ship built in Mystic, a circular drawing superimposed on a boat from a card compass used on a Noank fishing smack, and a whale oil forecastle lamp from a blacksmith shop in Groton.

This seal was used for many years, and in November 1963 the present Town seal was designed and adopted for use. The photographs below show the two different seals. *(April 8, 2005)*

1935 Groton seal, *left*, and 1963 Groton seal, *right*
(Courtesy Jim Steeter)

# The Groton Town Clerk's Office at the Avery Homestead

A name embedded in the history of Groton is Avery. It is said that Captain James Avery, who was born in 1620, came to our country along with John Winthrop in 1630. In 1657, Captain Avery and his family moved to the east side of the Thames River and settled in Poquonnock Plain. He built a house on his farm, which stretched from the "great brook," subsequently named the Poquonnock River, to the "three rocks," which are the ledges located on the east side of Claude Chester School. In 1705, when Groton became a town unto itself, Avery's oldest son, Samuel, became Groton's first townsman.

In 1657, Edward Stallion, a stalwart mariner and trader, bought land on Birch Plain, the area of Groton where several shopping centers are located today. He subsequently built a home on land located near the intersections of Poquonnock Road and Long Hill Road (Route 1). In 1670, Stallion and his wife, Margarett, gave the house and property to their daughter Debora(h) as a wedding gift after she married James Avery, Jr., the son of Captain Avery.

Throughout those years many additions were made to the small original house. One noteworthy addition was made in 1684 after James Avery, Jr., bought the old Blinman church in New London and subsequently used the materials from the structure to add a wing to the west side of his home in Groton. Modifications and additions were made to the structure in an almost haphazard fashion. The house took on an appearance of uniqueness when a separate two-story addition, with a second chimney, was added to one end of the building and a lean-to was added to the other end.

Over the next 220-plus years, eight successive generations of Averys resided in the house, and it became known as "the Hive of the Averys." Eventually, the house became the property of James Denison Avery, who was the great-grandson of Lieutenant Parke Avery, who had fought and lost an eye in the Battle of Fort Griswold.

James D. Avery was elected town clerk of Groton in 1874 and, as was the custom, he kept all town records, dating back to 1703, at his home, and all town business was conducted there, as there was no town hall. Fortunately for Groton, as will be mentioned later, Avery kept most of the records in two large fireproof safes in the house.

On the night of July 20, 1894, sparks from a passing locomotive, on railroad tracks located near the house, landed on the west roof of the house. The age of the wooden house, and the fact that Groton had been experiencing a very hot and dry summer, made the house an easy prey to the fire.

The "Hive of the Avery House" prior to its burning
(Courtesy Mystic River Historical Society)

After ensuring that his family members were safely out, Avery picked up some of the more recent records to carry from the house and then shut the doors to the safes. Within a short thirty minutes the landmark structure had been reduced to ashes, with only the two stone chimneys and the two safes remaining standing. Unfortunately, all abstracts and road charts were not in the safes and were destroyed by the fire.

It took four days for the safes to cool down enough to enable representatives from the safe company to open them. Once opened, a total of forty-six books were discovered. Five of the books were completely unharmed and, except for the leather bindings on the remaining books being melted, all of the contents of the records were found to be in good condition. The books with the damaged binders were subsequently rebound at a cost of about $10 per book.

Although the fire had destroyed what was believed to be the oldest dwelling house in the town that was still standing on its original foundations, the Town can be thankful that Town Clerk Avery had the forethought to have acquired the fireproof safes to store most of the town's significant and historic records. *(June 12, 2008)*

# Land Records Building

Groton's first Town Clerk and Land Records building was built in 1895 by Nelson Morgan, at his own expense, after he was elected town clerk. It was located at Morgan's Corner, or, as it is known today, the intersection of North Road and Route 1 (Fort Hill Road), and was situated where the present Johnson's Hardware store is located. The two-room wooden building remained in operation until the new Groton Town Hall opened in September of 1908. Approximately eight months after the clerk's office moved to the new facilities, the old building was moved to Center Groton, where it was converted into a private residence. It was subsequently destroyed by fire. *(March 18, 2005)*

Groton's old Land Records Building
(Courtesy Jim Streeter)

# Groton's First Meeting House

Groton's first "Meeting House" was a two-story wooden building located on the top of Fort Hill. In 1845, the building was purchased from the Second Baptist Church for the price of $225. It continued to be used as the town's Meeting House for approximately sixty years. In 1907, Morton F. Plant, one of Groton's most affluent and prominent citizens, made a generous offer to erect, at his expense, a new Town Hall. He stipulated that the building be used to house the Town Clerk's office and the probate office. In September 1908, construction of the new Town Hall was completed at a cost of a little over $24,000. The building still houses the clerk's and probate offices. This is a picture of Groton's first Meeting House. *(August 19, 2005)*

Groton's first Meeting House
(Courtesy Robert Bankel)

# Changes in Groton's Form of Government

As part of the November 2009 election, residents of Groton voted in favor of revisions to the town's charter. Some residents had suggested that the charter include a "budget referendum" process wherein the public could vote to approve or disapprove a budget proposed by the Town Council and/or Board of Education. Although this recommendation was taken under consideration, the Charter Revision Committee voted not to include this in the updated charter. A "Budget Referendum" of sorts was, at one time, an intricate part of Groton's government process.

From its beginning in 1705 and continuing for 250 years, the Town of Groton operated under what was known as a "Board of Selectmen–town meeting" form of government. In this type of governmental structure, the legislative power of the Town was vested in the "Town Meeting," which was comprised of as many or as few voters that chose to attend a scheduled meeting. A three-member "Board of Selectmen," elected by the voters, also possessed some policy-making powers; however, their main function was to serve as the chief administrative authority of the Town. The chairman of this board was the only full-time member and was generally considered to be the town's chief executive officer. He had limited powers, and before he could act on any matter, he needed the approval of either the Second or Third Selectmen.

The Selectmen were responsible for supervising the daily affairs of the Town, which included public works, highways, public safety, welfare, health, parks and recreation. They were also responsible for compiling preliminary budget requests and administering the annual budget. They were responsible for making appointments to the various Town commissions, boards, and committees.

As a point of interest, it should be noted that two regular Town Meetings were held each year; a budget meeting was held in May and a regular business meeting in September. Special meetings were held as necessary. The budget meeting was paramount to a "Budget Referendum."

The town meeting–selectmen form of government was designed for a small town where the duties of office were simple enough to be performed by part-time officials. Between the period of 1940 and 1950, the population of Groton had increased dramatically, from approximately 10,900 to over 25,000. The rapid growth in population in conjunction with an upswing in business and industrial activities made the governing and budget processes more complex. One would think that there would have been an increase in attendance at the town meetings; however, this was not the case. The annual business meeting held in 1954 attracted only 30 voters. In 1953, 1954, and 1955, the turnout for the annual budget meeting was approximately 150 voters each year. At a special meeting in May of 1954, called to consider an $800,000 school bond issue, only 13 voters attended. Increasingly, the selectmen and many residents felt the town meeting form of government had become outmoded.

On January 8, 1953, at a special town meeting, a committee was appointed by the voters "to investigate all town affairs for the purpose of making a recommendation on whether or not a different form of town government would be more beneficial to the citizens." The committee, which took on the name "Committee of 19" from the number of members it had, conducted a two-and-a-half-year study of the town and the efficiency of its government. The final recommendation of this committee was to establish a "Town Manager–Town Council" form of government.

At a town meeting held on October 10, 1955, attended by four hundred voters, a committee was elected to draft a new charter to include a change in the town's form of government. Attendees at the meeting voted to broaden the scope of the charter committee by directing them to draft several different charters, outlining not only the "Town Manager–Town Council" form of government but also a "Town Manager–Representative Town Meeting," or a combination of both forms of government.

On January 19, 1957, a referendum was held providing the voters with the choice between the "Town Manager–Town Council" or the "Town Manager – Town Council – Representative Town Meeting" form of government. Voter turnout was disheartening, with only 4.8 percent of the 9,000 eligible citizens coming to the polls. The "Town Manager–Town Council–Representative Town Meeting" form of government passed by a vote of 256 to 183.

Groton's new charter, including its new form of government, was presented to the State Legislature for approval. It was subsequently passed with minor changes and signed into law by Governor Abraham Ribicoff on May 10, 1957.

Although some residents feel that Groton's form of government is too complex and cumbersome, the bottom line is that it contains good checks and balances, but, more importantly, *it works. (February 19, 2009)*

# *Groton Elections One Hundred Years Ago*

With municipal elections just a few days away, I thought it might be interesting to go back one hundred years to see what the Groton elections were like back then.

I think it would be best to start by explaining the election process as it is today and then discussing what it was like back in 1907. One must remember that there are strict Connecticut state laws that provide specific rules governing the election process.

During the week of July 17th through the 24th of this year, Groton's Republican and Democratic Committees held special meetings, called caucuses, to nominate and endorse candidates to run for various elected Town offices to be held on November 6th . If my calculations are correct, there are between 104 and 112 days between the time a person is selected to run and the date that he or she is elected. Of course there are numerous administrative electoral things, such as primary elections, voter registration, absentee ballots, etc., that may transpire during this period of time, but, basically, the campaign begins once the caucuses are held.

Once the campaign begins in earnest, candidates begin their "door-to-door" campaigns, mail voters their biographical and platform literature, and have political ads placed in local newspapers. Also, thirty days prior to the election, in accordance with town regulations, they post individual political yard signs. As the election nears, the political parties and the candidates often contact voters via telephone seeking their endorsement. Needless to say, the campaign process can be very taxing and expensive for the political parties and candidates. The process can also be annoying to the voters.

In conducting research into the Town of Groton elections held one hundred years ago, I guess you could say that I was shocked at the process utilized back then.

According to newspaper accounts, the party caucuses that year were held on September 30th. Nominations were made for the following positions: selectmen, assessors, town clerk, board of relief, tax collector, agents for the town deposit fund, auditors, constables, registrars, school visitors, treasurer, and tree warden. Quite a "lineup" of positions.

The Republican Party held the majority of these positions before the election that year, and it was expected that they would maintain most of the seats after the election.

The "hottest" issue during the campaign was the race for the town clerkship position. Republican George F. Costello was running against Democrat Henry L. Bailey, and it was believed that Costello would receive an overwhelming majority of the votes over Bailey.

Immediately after the caucuses were held, the various nominees and their friends were said to have "commenced to get busy and to campaign in earnest, hustling votes."

The primary explanation for the quickness of starting the campaign was probably the fact that the election was held on October 7th. Yes, that's correct, just *one week* after the caucuses. Not a sufficient time to permit mailing out fliers or posting yard signs. Of course making telephone solicitation calls was extremely limited, and placing a political ad in the *Day* newspaper was very costly. Fortunately, there was great interest in the election within the community and the voters appreciated door-to-door campaigning.

When the election was over, the Republicans had maintained their majority control, but Democratic candidate Henry L. Bailey had surprisingly beaten his Republican foe for the clerk's position.

Oh, by the way, I could only find one political advertisement in the *Day* newspaper in the week preceding the election, and it was for the tax collections position. On the other hand, I did find that a business ad for "Coe & Bailey" grocers appeared directly below each news article about the upcoming election. Coincidence or just good political savvy?

I am sure there is pro and con to reverting back to having the elections one week after the party caucuses; however, just imagine the time and money that could be saved and redirected toward other important civic causes. Just some "food for thought." *(November 1, 2007)*

# Chapter 2

## Maritime and Lighthouses

# Naval Submarine Base New London (Groton)

The Naval Submarine Base New London, which is located in Groton, had its beginning as a naval station back in 1868. The "Navy Yard," as it was called, was first used as a depot for docking and laying-up ships that were not in service. In the early 1900s, a coaling station was established at the Yard to refuel various ships traveling through the waters of New England. In 1912, due to the lack of anticipated refueling activity, consideration was given to disposal of the naval station.

Fortunately for Groton, the station never closed, and studies were undertaken to transpose the Yard into a "Submarine Base."

On October 18, 1915, ninety years ago this week, six submarines, accompanied by two tenders and one torpedo boat destroyer, arrived in Groton to open the new submarine base. The submarines G-1, G-2, and G-4 were assigned to the tender *Ozark* and the E-1, D-1, and D-3 were assigned to the tender *Tonapah*. *Columbia* was the name of the destroyer.

In 1916, a school was established on the station to train submariners, and in 1917, the Navy decided to use the station exclusively for submarines. Thus the beginning of the New London Submarine Base.

The Base has continued to develop over the years to become the core of our nation's undersea warfare. A member of the federal Base Realignment and Closure Commission recently described the Base as "a center of excellence for submarine warfare." *(October 21, 2005)*

19

# Groton's Mammoth Steamships
## (Part I)

As many local residents recently scurried to the banks of the Thames River to get a glimpse of the "monster" cruise ship visiting the port of New London, I think it is important that we turn back the pages of history to the time when Groton gathered world attention when its Eastern Shipbuilding Company built what was then considered the world's largest ships.

In 1900, James J. Hill, internationally known for building the Great Northern & Northern Pacific Railways and for incorporating the Great Northern Steamship Company, conceived the idea of shipping large amounts of wheat to China and Japan to supplement their diets of rice. He learned that the Japanese Navigation Company, the third-largest steamship company in the world, had been shipping grain, lumber, cotton, steel rails, tobacco, and silver to China and Japan; however, their boats were inadequate in size to handle the shipments. Hill, who was known as "The Empire Builder," felt that with the proper size vessels, he would have no problem capturing this prospective wealthy shipping market. He in turn contracted with the Eastern Shipbuilding Company to build two steamships that would be the largest freight and passenger boats ever built. These ships would not only be capable of shipping large amounts of cargo but would also permit carrying over three thousand passengers and crew.

When Hill awarded the contracts, the Eastern Shipbuilding Company did not have facilities large enough to build the ships. Charles Hanscom, president of Eastern Shipbuilding, who had recently resigned his position as general superintendent of the Bath Iron Works in Maine, immediately started searching for an appropriate location to build the vessels. Ultimately, he selected the property on the Groton bank of the Thames River that had previously been used as the terminal for the Providence and Boston railroad for transporting train cars, via ferry, between Groton and New London. The ferry facility had ceased operation in the late 1880s after the first railroad bridge was built across the Thames. Hanscom, upon inspecting the former ferry property (consisting of approximately forty acres and having approximately one half a mile waterfront), considered it ideal for his Eastern Shipbuilding Company to build Hill's mammoth steamships.

Incidentally, in 1910 the New London Ship and Engine Company took over the shipyard from Eastern, and ultimately it became the home of the Electric Boat Company.

Construction on the twin-screw steamships SS *Minnesota* and SS *Dakota*, names selected by Mr. Hill, began in early 1901. The shipyard employed well over two thousand, making it, at the time, one of the largest employers in New England. The construction of these ships contributed to a commercial and industrial boom in Groton and New London.

The *Minnesota* was launched on April 16, 1903, and placed into service in August of 1904. The *Dakota* was launched in February 1904 and made its maiden voyage in September 1905. Total cost to build the two ships was placed at approximately $7,900,000.

When built, these steamships were considered the largest ships in the world. They were 630 feet in length, 73 feet 6 inches wide, and were 56 feet high to the upper deck, 88 feet high to the captain's bridge, and 177 feet high to the top of the highest mast. From the outer bottom of the ship to her navigating bridge were 11 steel-plated decks or platforms. They displaced 40,000 tons, or 230 tons greater than the then White Star liner Cedric.

Although primarily cargo vessels, the *Minnesota* and *Dakota* had accommodations for 172 first-class passengers, 110 second-class passengers, 68 third-class passengers, 2,424 troops or steerage, and 250 crew members. The ships had a total cargo capacity of approximately 30,000 tons, which was equivalent to the cargo capacity of 100 trains of 25 cars each. The vessels were twice as large as modern battleships of the time and could carry ten full regiments with their equipment.

The ship's engines produced 12,000 horsepower, which enabled a speed of 14 knots. It was necessary for the ships to take on more than 5,000 tons of coal and 8,000 tons of water for their own consumption on a single trip.

Needless to say, the ships were "mastodons" in size, and the launching of these vessels were spectacular events. Particulars about the launch ceremonies will be the subject of next week's article. *(July 17, 2008)*

The SS *Minnesota*
(Courtesy Carol Kimball)

# Groton's Mammoth Steamships
# (Part II)


# The Launchings


Last week's article discussed the establishment in 1900 of Groton's Eastern Shipbuilding Company and the construction of two steamships by that company, the *Minnesota* and the *Dakota*, which, at that time, were considered to be the largest ships in the world.

Just as the task of building these monster ships was a tremendous undertaking, the preparations for their launchings were also elaborate and monumental. The launching of the *Minnesota*, the first ship to be launched, was held on April 16, 1903. It was such a spectacular event that an unofficial "holiday" of sorts was declared throughout New London County.

To begin with, the total cost of preparing the ship for launch, including labor and material, was placed at about $50,000. The ship had been built on a bed of eight hundred thousand board feet of lumber, which was said to be a sufficient amount of wood to stock a small lumberyard at a cost of approximately $20,000. It was necessary to raise the ship from the bed of lumber to enable her to slide down the launching ways. This was accomplished by inserting and ramming two hundred hardwood wedges between the ship and the wooden bed, about every four feet on each side of the boat. To help the ship slide down the ways, an estimated twelve tons of special grease was applied to the ways. The cost of the grease was placed at nearly $2,500.

It was estimated that over forty thousand spectators were present at the launching, which was said to have attracted the most individuals to the area since the Centennial Day celebration on September 6, 1881. Just about every business in Groton and New London closed for at least half the day to enable their employees to witness the historic event.

Trains with special cars attached to regular trains, full to their capacity, arrived from Westerly, Stonington, Mystic, Norwich, Putnam, and New London. Special cars were also attached to the regular Boston express to bring guests to the launching.

A fifteen-hundred-seat grandstand was erected directly opposite the main gate of the shipbuilding company, from which an unobstructed view of the launching could be seen. Tickets for seats in the grandstand were sold out two days in advance. Although the exact cost of a spectator seat in this grandstand could not be ascertained, I am sure it was a handsome amount, especially in light of the fact that tickets for spectator ferries and seats on nearby private properties overlooking the shipyard were selling at 50 cents for adults and 25 cents for children.

Dignitaries attending the event included then Governor Abiram Chamberlain and almost everyone of note who was connected with the State General Assembly. Others in attendance included members of the Board of Trade, the Court of Common Council, the State Judiciary Committee, and the Connecticut Mayors Association. Many of the dignitaries viewed the launch from the steamer *Block Island*, which had been chartered by the New London Board of Trade. It was estimated that there were over twelve hundred spectators on this craft.

Weather-wise, it was not an ideal day for the launch. The area had been experiencing a northeaster storm over the previous two days, causing cloudy skies, a northeast wind, and unusually cold temperatures. For those who had arrived hours prior to the 12:20 PM scheduled launch, the cold had "chilled them to the bone." Many spectators wore heavy winter coats and gloves.

Unfortunately, due to bothersome bilge blocks, the launching was delayed almost two hours. At 2:15 PM, Mrs. Clara Hill, daughter of James J. Hill, who had commissioned the Eastern Shipyard Company to build the mammoth steamships, christened the *Minnesota* with the traditional bottle of wine.

With the blowing of ships' whistles and thunderous cheers from the crowd, the *Minnesota* gracefully and slowly slid down the ways into the Thames River. As her stern struck the water, there was a tremendous splash, sending a mighty wave up and down the river. As the boat traveled toward New London, her momentum was checked by anchors and three tugboats. The *Minnesota*, the greatest and largest steamship in the world, was now a reality.

The thrilling launching of the *Minnesota*, and later the *Dakota*, brought international attention to Groton. Initially the SS *Minnesota* and SS *Dakota* brought new life to shipping services between the United States and the Orient; within a few short years unexpected and unfortunate circumstances caused the demise of these ships. Next week's article will detail those circumstances. *(July 24, 2008)*

# Groton's Mammoth Steamships
# (Part III)

## Their Demise

This is the concluding part of the series detailing the two monster-size freight and passenger steamships built in the early 1900s at Groton's newly established Eastern Shipbuilding Company. At the time, these vessels, the SS *Minnesota* and the SS *Dakota*, were considered to be the largest ships in the world.

The ships were contracted by James J. Hill, who was internationally known for building the Great Northern and Northern Pacific Railways and for incorporating the Great North Steamship Company. He was also known throughout the business world as "The Empire Builder." Hill had originally conceived the idea of shipping large amounts of wheat to China and Japan to supplement their diets of rice. He subsequently learned that Japan had been attempting to ship not only grain, but also lumber, cotton, steel rails, tobacco, and silver throughout the Orient; however, their boats were inadequate in size to handle the shipments. Believing that, with the proper size vessels, he would have no problem capturing this prospectively wealthy shipping market, Hill decided to build two steamships that would be the largest freight and passenger boats ever built.

The *Minnesota* was launched on April 16, 1903, and placed into service in August of 1904. The *Dakota* was launched in February 1904 and made its maiden voyage in September 1905.[*]

The ships had a total cargo capacity of approximately thirty thousand tons, which was equivalent to the cargo capacity of one hundred trains of twenty-five cars each. They could also accommodate over three thousand passengers and crew.

The *Minnesota*, on her maiden voyage on January 22, 1905, departed Seattle, Washington, and sailed to Asia with three hundred passengers and the largest cargo said to have ever crossed the Pacific

Ocean. The twenty-eight thousand tons of cargo, valued at over $1.2 million, consisted of everything from pins to tobacco and cotton. The ship made calls at Yokohama, Kobe, Nagasaki, Shanghai, Manila, and Hong Kong.

This vessel made forty round trips between the West Coast of the United States and the Far East between January 1905 and October 1915. Unfortunately, the *Minnesota* was too large for the volume of business available, and she never made money. Another condition not taken into consideration when the ships were being built for trade in the Orient, especially Japan, was the insufficient amount of coal available that was needed for the return trip. The ships required five thousand tons of coal for a single round trip to the Orient.

In November 1915, while on a voyage, boilers on the *Minnesota* had to be replaced. Some say they just gave out, and others say it was sabotage. Whatever the case, it was necessary to replace the boilers, and the ship spent all of 1916 being repaired, a very costly venture.

In 1917, she was purchased by the British government for service in World War I. In 1919, she was chartered by the Navy, renamed *Troy,* and converted to a troop transport. She made three passages from France to the United States and brought home more than fourteen thousand veterans from the "Great War."

She was decommissioned in 1919 and again became the *Minnesota.* She never resumed active service and was sold for scrap in November 1923.

The *Dakota* did not have as long a life span as the *Minnesota.* She made her maiden voyage from Seattle on September 20, 1905. On March 3, 1907, while on her seventh journey, forty miles south of Yokohama, Japan, for reasons unknown, the captain of the *Dakota* steered the ship into an area widely avoided by mariners because of an abundance of treacherous reefs. The ship struck the Shira Hami Reef. The 726 passengers and crew of the ship were rescued, and the vessel remained partially sunk until March 23, when she broke in half and sank.

Although Mr. Hill's idea of building the two mammoth steamships did not reap the financial benefits as first thought, it can be said that some greatness did come as a result of the building of these ships. The shipyard where the *Minnesota* and *Dakota* were constructed was subsequently purchased by the New London Ship & Engine Company and then the Electric Boat Company. It is this shipyard, and its many dedicated workers, that contributed proudly to Groton being considered the "Submarine Capital of the World." *(July 31, 2008)*

# First Submarines Built in Groton

While having a coffee at a local restaurant a few weeks ago, I overheard some young men discussing the history of what is now known as the Electric Boat Corporation, referred to by many of us Grotonites as "EB." As they continued their conversation, my ears perked when they mentioned that the first submarine built in Groton was the USS *Cuttlefish*. On my best behavior, and of course in a most diplomatic fashion, I introduced myself to the gentlemen and explained that the *Cuttlefish* was indeed the first submarine built for the United States Navy in Groton, but it was not the first submarine built here. With their interest piqued, I relayed what I knew about the submarine(s) that were built at EB prior to the *Cuttlefish*.

I explained that "EB" in Groton had its beginning in 1911 when the Electric Boat Company of New Jersey acquired the New London Ship and Engine Company (NELSECO) in Groton to build diesel engines, machinery, and parts for submarines. The NELSECO shipyard was located where the present Electric Boat Corporation is situated.

In 1922, Electric Boat expanded the facilities at the NELSECO yard to assist in overhauling thirty S-Class submarines The overhauls entailed rebuilding the engines and installing torpedo tubes on the boats.

In November 1924, the Electric Boat Company signed a contract with the government of Peru to build two submarines for the South American republic and a number of torpedoes. They also were to construct a naval submarine base in Callao, Peru. The submarines themselves were to be completely constructed at the NELSECO Yard in Groton. The cost to build each of the subs was approximately $1,220,000, with an additional cost of about $260,000 for the torpedoes and associated accessory items totaling over $260,000. Over five hundred employees were added to the payroll at the yard as a result of the contract.

The submarines were of the Holland-type design. At two hundred feet in length, and displacing approximately eight hundred tons, they were somewhat larger that the U.S. Navy's R-type submarine and smaller than the S-type. Each was powered by two NELSECO diesel engines, which provided a top speed of 14.5 knots. The vessels had a cruising radius of about eight thousand miles. Both ships were armed with four torpedo tubes and a three-inch .50-caliber gun.

The keels for the submarines, named *R-1* and *R-2*, were both laid on February 25, 1925. Miss Isabel Leguia, the daughter of Peruvian President Augusto B. Leguia, christened the keel of the *R-1*, and Mrs. Clark Woodward, wife of Admiral Woodward, the chief of the American Naval Mission in Peru, christened the *R-2*. Approximately one thousand guests, including officials from the United States and Peru and employees of the shipyard, attended the ceremony.

On April 29, 1926, the Peruvian Sub *R-2* was launched. Mrs. Woodward, the original sponsor, was unable to attend, and Mrs. Enriqua Monge, the wife of the chief of the Peruvian Naval Commission, christened the submarine. No explanation could be found as to why the *R-2* was launched prior to the *R-1*. Incidentally, a bottle of Peruvian wine was used to launch the vessel. Over fifteen hundred attended the ceremony. The boat was delivered to the Peruvian government on July 31st.

On July 12, 1926, the *R-1* was launched. Nearly two thousand spectators assembled for the ceremony. Mrs. Maria Meyer Ontaneda, wife of the commander of the *R-2*, christened this vessel. It was delivered on October 4th.

The Peruvian government was so pleased with the submarines constructed at the Groton Yard that by early December of 1926 another contract was awarded to the Electric Boat Company to have two additional submarines built at NELSECO.

By the way, the *Cuttlefish* was launched at the Groton shipyard on November 21, 1933. *(March 5, 2009)*

The *R-2* submarine on the Thames River
(Courtesy Carol Kimball)

# Electric Boat and PT Boats

Many individuals are under the impression that the Electric Boat Division of Groton produced Patrol Torpedo (PT) Boats. Well, there is some truth to the matter.

Beginning in 1940 and continuing to the latter part of 1945, the Electric Launch Company, better known as "Elco," of Bayonne, New Jersey, built almost 399 of these famous torpedo boats for the United States Navy. At the peak of production, one PT boat was built every sixty hours. The boat was constructed of double-planked mahogany over a wooden frame. At the end of the World War II, Elco merged with its sister company, the Electric Boat Company in Groton.

In June of 1949, the Electric Boat Company was awarded a contract to design and build *PT-809*, one of four experimental torpedo boats to be built of aluminum. When completed in February 1951, *PT-809* was ninety-eight feet six inches in length and weighed ninety-five tons. She was originally assigned duties at the Fifth Naval District MTB (Motor Torpedo Boat) Detail in Norfolk, Virginia.

In 1959, *PT-809* was modified and assigned duties as an escort to presidential yachts. She was renamed the *Guardian* and assigned to the Naval Administrative Unit at the Naval Gun Factory in Washington, DC. During her duty as a presidential yacht escort, she provided escort services to President Dwight D. Eisenhower's yacht *Barbara Ann* and President John F. Kennedy's yacht *Honey Fitz*.

After her White House duties, she was reassigned to the Navy Amphibious Base Little Creek in Norfolk, Virginia, and renamed *Retriever*. She was used to transport, launch, and recover drone torpedoes for fleet training. She was taken out of service in 1988.

It has been reported that in 1993 Electric Boat's *PT-809* was cut up by a scrap company for salvage value of its aluminum. **(July 20, 2006)**

# Tales of the USS Groton

In October 1976, Groton was honored when the nuclear submarine *Groton* (*SSN 694*) was launched at the Electric Boat Division. Many individuals were under the impression that this was the first ship named after Groton.

Actually, the first ship to bear the name USS *Groton* was a Tacoma-class frigate, which was built at the Butler Shipbuilding Company in Superior, Wisconsin. Designated as a "patrol frigate," *PF-29*, it was launched on September 14, 1943. The fifteen-hundred-ton boat was approximately 304 feet in length and had a beam of 37½ feet. It was built at a cost of $1,740,000. Incidentally the ship was equipped to have the following armament: two 3"/50 dual purpose gun mounts, two twin 409 mm gun mounts, nine 20 mm guns, one Hedgehog depth charge projector, eight Y-gun depth charge projects, and two depth charge racks.

Interestingly, it was the tenth Navy frigate to be launched at the Butler shipyard within sixty-three days.

Mrs. Percy Palmer of Groton Long Point, accompanied by her husband, represented the Town of Groton at the launching ceremony. She was selected to be the sponsor of the ship as the mother of a Navy hero, Bruce Davis Palmer, who had lost his life in the sinking of the Navy's light cruiser USS *Juneau* by a Japanese submarine in the Pacific theater on November 13, 1942.

Mrs. Palmer presented the ship with a silver water pitcher as a gift from the Town of Groton to commemorate the launching.

The Frigate USS *Groton* was commissioned in September 1944 and served in the North Atlantic as a weather station craft providing important reports to Allied weather stations to help guide wartime traffic safely to Europe. The ship remained on duty, based in Argentia, Newfoundland, until February 1945, when she returned to Boston, Massachusetts, and, interestingly, was transferred to the United States Coast Guard. The ship was simultaneously decommissioned from the United States Navy and recommissioned in the Coast Guard in March of 1946 and designated the USCGC *Groton* (*PF-29*). She was again assigned to weather duty off of Argentia until September 1946, when she was again decommissioned.

In January 1947, the USS *Groton* was turned over to the State Department for disposal, and in 1950 she was sold to the Government of Colombia in March of that year. She was renamed the A.R.C. *Almirante Padilla* and served distinguishingly with the United Nations forces off the shores of Korea. In 1952, she became a training ship, and, according to a *Day* news article, "she became a sort of symbol for Colombians and was often used by businessmen there as a trademark, much like the *Nautilus* was used in [America]."

In June of 1964, the *Padilla* went aground in Colombian waters and was declared unsalvageable. The United States Navy Submarine Rescue Vessel *Sunbird*, at the request of the Colombian government, helped to destroy the ship. Before the former USS *Groton* was scuttled, a few items, including the [Groton] water pitcher, were saved from the ship.

In August 1964, the water pitcher was presented to Groton Town Mayor Thomas Hagerty, along with a letter from Colombian Naval Fleet Captain Jaime Parra Ramierz, which stated, "The frigate ex-USS *Groton* has been a loyal guardian of the ideals of the free world, regardless of which flag she sailed." Not only was that statement a great tribute to our country and the United States Navy but also made Groton extremely proud of its namesake. *(September 13, 2007)*

The first ship named *Groton*
(Courtesy Jim Streeter)

# The Avery Point Lighthouse

With the relighting and rededication ceremony of the Avery Point Lighthouse only three days away, it might be appropriate to relay some little-known facts about this historic structure.

The lighthouse is situated at the southeastern end of the University of Connecticut's Avery Point campus in Groton. The campus property was originally the site of the seventy-two-acre estate of Groton's wealthy industrialist and philanthropist, Morton F. Plant.

In 1938, some two decades after the death of Mr. Plant, his estate was sold at auction to the State of Connecticut.

In March of 1942, the property was sold by the State of Connecticut to the United States Government. The quit claim deed for the transfer of land stipulated that within a period of five years, the "United States of America [would] erect and maintain on or over the land ... beacon lights or other buildings and apparatus to be used in aid of navigation" or in more specific terms, a lighthouse.

In 1942, the United States Coast Guard (USCG) occupied the site and established the Coast Guard Training Station.

In March of 1943, the Coast Guard fulfilled the requirement of the quit claim deed and completed the construction of the Avery Point Lighthouse. Although at the time it was considered "ready for service," due to World War II "hostility concerns," it was not lit until May 2, 1944.

The lighthouse was an official aid to navigation and was first listed on the Coast Guard's [navigational] List of Lights from 1944 through 1967. It also appears on various USCG approved navigation and maritime charts. Initially the beacon of the lighthouse was a cluster of eight white lights; however, in 1960, at the request of the Shennecossett Yacht Club, the characteristic was changed to flashing green every four seconds.

The Avery Point Lighthouse shortly after being built.
(Courtesy Jim Streeter)

In 1967, the Coast Guard closed its training center at Avery Point and moved to New York. The light was extinguished, and the property was again occupied by the State of Connecticut. It subsequently became a sub-campus of the University of Connecticut.

Unfortunately, over the next thirty-plus years, maintenance and upkeep of the lighthouse was sorely lacking and largely discontinued. The structure developed serious deterioration problems, and in 1997 consideration was given to raze the structure.

Fortunately, thanks to the efforts of a group of local citizens calling themselves the Avery Point Lighthouse Society (APLS), the structure was saved from the wrecking ball.

Over the past six years, APLS, which is a chapter of the American Lighthouse Foundation, and the University of Connecticut have worked together in an effort to save, restore, and relight the lighthouse. Thanks to a determined effort on the part of APLS and UCONN the lighthouse has been restored to its original glory. It has also been placed on the National Register of Historic Places. The lighthouse beacon will be relit on October 15th and placed back in service as an official aid to navigation. *(October 12, 2006)*

# Ram Island Lightship

Although Groton is fortunate to have three lighthouses within its boundaries (Avery Point, Morgan Point, and New London Ledge), very few individuals realize that a lightship was moored off of Ram Island in Fishers Island Sound off shore of Noank from 1886 through 1925. Lightships were often positioned in areas where water levels were too deep or where a lighthouse would be too expensive or impractical to construct.

The lightship, called *Ram Island Lightship* and designated *LV 23*, served as a beacon and an aid to navigation for steamers and other maritime traffic traveling through Fishers Island Sound from Stonington to New York. The wooden vessel was 95½ feet in length, with a 25-foot beam and weighed 203 tons. Lanterns, each equipped with eight oil lamps, were affixed to the ship's two masts. A hand-operated 667-pound bell was used for a fog signal. It had a crew of a captain, a mate, four seamen, and a cook.

In April 1925, the ship was replaced with a lighted bell buoy. *(April 29, 2005)*

Ram Island Lightship with a supply tender ship tied up to her.
(Courtesy Jim Streeter)

# Morgan Point Lighthouse

In the early 1830s, the United States government wanted to build a lighthouse on the west side of the mouth of the Mystic River to assist mariners entering the river. In 1831, Noank shipbuilder Roswell Avery Morgan sold to the federal government the land known today as Morgan Point.

Little known to many people is the fact that there have been two lighthouses built on Morgan Point. The first structure, a twenty-five-foot white granite tower, was built in 1931 at a cost of approximately $4,200. Ten lamps and reflectors were used for its beacon. A separate six-room "keepers" house was built approximately eighty feet from the tower.

In 1868, due to decaying of the original structure and the desire of the government to replace the ten-lamp beacon with a more modern and powerful beacon lens, a new lighthouse was constructed. The new lighthouse was a two-story, eight-room granite structure having a cast-iron light tower attached to the front of the building, sixty-one feet above the ocean. Cost to build the second structure was approximately $11,800. The lighthouse beacon remained in operation until 1921, when it was replaced by a gas-powered automatic light on top of a granite day marker at the mouth of the river. The lantern room on the lighthouse was subsequently removed and, in 1922, the lighthouse was sold at auction.

Some interesting facts about the Morgan Point Lighthouses concern women who became lighthouse keepers. During the period of 1838 through 1854, Eliza Daboll took over the light-keeping responsibilities after the death of her husband, Ezra. In 1869, Francis McDonald became the light keeper for the second lighthouse after her husband became ill and had to move to Florida. She remained keeper for a period of approximately three years, until she too moved to Florida.
*(September 30, 2005)*

The second Morgan Point Lighthouse prior to 1922
(Courtesy Jim Streeter)

# Groton's New London Ledge Lighthouse

Many readers of my articles are aware of my involvement in saving, preserving, and restoring America's lighthouses, specifically those in New England. A few years ago, after being made aware that New London Ledge Lighthouse was in need of major repair, I offered to lend my assistance. I was subsequently appointed to the Board of Directors of the New London Ledge Lighthouse Foundation.

Although the lighthouse has for many years been construed as being located in New London, according to official U.S. Coast Guard navigational charts, it is actually situated in Groton waters. I guess you might say it falls in the same category as the "Submarine Base New London" and the "Groton–New London Airport," both being in Groton, not New London.

Completed in 1909, the lighthouse was originally named Southwest Ledge; however, to avoid confusion with a lighthouse having the same name in New Haven harbor, the name was changed to New London Ledge. To this day you can still find picture postcards identifying the lighthouse as Southwest Ledge.

Building of the lighthouse was authorized by the United States Senate in 1906, and in 1908 the contract to build the structure was awarded to the T. A. Scott Company of New London. Total cost allocated for the project was not to exceed $115,000.

Work on the lighthouse began on July 10, 1908, at the property owned by T. A. Scott on the Groton bank of the Thames River just south of the old railroad drawbridge where the former Spicer coaling dock was located. The first stage of construction was to build a large crib or form for the foundation of the lighthouse. The crib, measuring fifty-two feet square and approximately thirty-five feet high, was made of one hundred and sixty thousand board feet of yellow pine and nine tons of steel and iron.

On August 18, 1908, the crib was towed from its location in Groton to its final resting place on top of the Southwest Ledge at the mouth of the Thames River. The three-mile journey down river was no easy task. Three tugboats—the *T. A. Scott Jr.*, the *Harriet*, and the *Alert*—began towing the crib at five o'clock in the morning. At about ten o'clock, as the tide in the Thames began to recede, the crib, which drew a little over twenty-eight feet of water, grounded opposite the old Griswold Hotel. A fourth tug was added to the crew, and after the tide rose again, the crib continued to its final location. The entire trip took eight hours.

Once in position above Southwest Ledge, the crib was filled with rock riprap and approximately thirty-five hundred barrels of cement and sunk in twenty-eight feet of water. A riprap deposit, eighty-two feet square and ten feet deep, was placed around the foundation to protect the crib.

A concrete pier, fifty feet square and eighteen feet high, was then built on top of the crib as a foundation for the lighthouse dwelling and station.

The Hamilton R. Douglas Company, a general contractor in New London, was subcontracted by T. A. Scott to build the lighthouse dwelling. The unique three-story, eleven-room brick and granite design of the house came about as a result of the request from several wealthy home owners on the nearby coast who wanted the lighthouse to be representative of the styles of their homes. Thus, an architectural design incorporating both Colonial Revival and French Second Empire was selected.

The lighthouse was originally equipped with a fourth-order Fresnel lens and a kerosene lamp. The characteristic of the beacon was three white flashes followed by a red flash every thirty seconds. The Fresnel lens was replaced in the mid-1980s with a newer electric optic. The old lens is on display at the New London Maritime Museum in the Customs House.

The lighthouse was placed in operation on November 10, 1909. It was manned by light keepers from its beginning through 1939 and then by U.S. Coast Guard personnel until the light was automated in 1987. In 1988, the New London Ledge Lighthouse Foundation, a nonprofit organization, received a thirty-year lease from the Coast Guard to take care of the structure.

Membership in the New London Ledge Lighthouse Foundation and interest in maintaining the lighthouse has dwindled over the past ten years. The lighthouse is presently in need of necessary maintenance and repair to keep it from falling into despair. The Foundation is in the process of reorganizing and is seeking support and membership.

Anyone interested in helping is encouraged to contact the Foundation at P.O. Box 855, New London, CT 06320. *(May 1, 2008)*

# The Haunting of New London Ledge Lighthouse

A few weeks ago, I wrote an article about the [Groton] New London Ledge Lighthouse. Many readers have reacted to the article by asking if there was any truth to the stories about the lighthouse being haunted by "Ernie the Ghost." Whether you believe in ghosts or not, the various stories about "Ernie" are certainly intriguing and entertaining but, more importantly, leave a great deal to one's imagination.

Purportedly, in the 1920s or 1930s, a light keeper named "Ernie" was assigned to the lighthouse. After learning that his wife had run off with the captain of the Block Island Ferry, he became so distraught he jumped or fell to his death from the roof of the lighthouse. Another version has him cutting his throat before he jumped to his death. Whatever the case, his body was never found, and he has subsequently haunted the lighthouse. It has been said that Ernie's haunting pranks have included opening and closing doors, washing floors, turning lights and the fog horn off and on, moving beds and removing sheets from them, knocking on walls, and untying boats at the lighthouse to set them adrift. He has also delighted in moving things around, especially in the room where he used to sleep when he was alive— "Ernie's Room."

Some of the versions of the story state that the suicide at the lighthouse took place in 1936 or 1938 and that Ernie's real name was John Randolf or Randolph.

Although I am not going to come right out and say that "Ernie" does not exist, I would like to relay some pieces of information I discovered while conducting research on the subject. It might be best to just list them and let the reader draw his or her conclusions.

    a.  No one named John Randolf (or Randolph) or "Ernie" is on the official list of light keepers assigned to the lighthouse from the time it was first lit in 1909 through 1939, when the United States Coast Guard took over keeper responsibilities.

    b.  The keeper assigned to the New London Ledge Lighthouse from 1926 through the time the Coast Guard took over was a Howard B. Beebe.

c. There are no notations in the lighthouse logbooks, or any other information relayed by Mr. Beebe, to indicate paranormal or unexplained activities taking place at the lighthouse while he was assigned there.

d. No entry was found in the lighthouse logs relating to the suicide or accidental death of anyone at the lighthouse.

e. No record was found in either the New London or Town of Groton clerk files recording the death of a John Randolf (or Randolph) during the period of 1909 through 1941.

f. There is no John Randolf (or Randolph) listed in the New London / Groton street directories for the period of 1920 through 1940.

g. The haunting activities are only mentioned by members of the Coast Guard after they assumed the lighthouse responsibilities in 1939.

h. Various paranormal investigative groups have conducted studies at the lighthouse; however, no significant unexplainable activities were noted or documented.

A few years ago, as part of a small volunteer work group, my wife and I spent the weekend at the lighthouse. We selected the area just outside of "Ernie's Room" as our sleeping quarters. Except for a member of our group donning a sheet and making ghostly cries, at no time did any of us experience any paranormal events. Maybe Ernie just took the night off?

Members of The Atlantic Paranormal Society (TAPS), who conducted intensive research at the lighthouse to identify and document any paranormal activities, concluded that there was "no evidence of haunting" at the lighthouse and that Ernie was "more lore than fact."

I am sure that, over the years, there have been some occurrences at the lighthouse that might lead a person to ask questions, and I personally believe that between those incidents and the lore of "Ernie the Ghost," a great deal of character and interest is brought to the lighthouse. Thus, I hope the story of Ernie will live on forever. *(June 5, 2008)*

New London Ledge Lighthouse around 1910
(Courtesy Jim Streeter)

# Lighthouse Tenders

Between the mid-1920s and early 1930s, the Electric Boat Company and its predecessor, the New London Ship & Engine Company, built various types of boats, including submarines, ferryboats, tugboats, and trawlers. In 1930, two lighthouse tenders, the *Althea* and the *Poinciana*, were built at the shipyard for the United States Lighthouse Service, which was subsequently incorporated into the responsibilities of the U.S. Coast Guard. The tenders were used to provide supplies and support to lighthouses and for servicing various maritime aids to navigation. Each was approximately eighty-one feet in length, displaced 120 tons, and was built at a cost of approximately $81,000.

Both boats were considered to be light draft bay and sound tenders designed for service in the inland waters of the South Atlantic coast. After being commissioned, the *Althea* was assigned to the Sixth Lighthouse District, based at Fort Pierce, Florida, and the *Poinciana* was assigned to the Seventh Lighthouse District, based at Key West, Florida. In October 1952, the *Althea* and the *Poinciana* both assisted in hurricane evacuations in Florida. Both tenders remained in service until 1962 and were subsequently sold for private use. The *Althea* became the M/V *Little Red* and the *Poinciana* became *Red's Baby*. (*March 30, 2006*)

The Lighthouse Tender *Althea*
(Courtesy Jim Streeter)

# Chapter 3

---

# People to Remember

# Our State Flag

## Abby Slocomb

Did you know that the design for the Connecticut state flag had its beginning in Groton?

In 1895, Abby Slocomb, who was a member of Groton's Anna Warner Bailey Chapter of the Daughters of the American Revolution, was appointed as the chairman of the Fort Griswold Monument House Committee.

Shortly after becoming the chairman, Mrs. Slocomb felt it would be nice to decorate the inside of the building with the state's flag. It was at this time she was informed that there were at least thirty-five different flags in existence being used by various Connecticut troops and that none had been adopted by the General Assembly as Connecticut's state flag.

Mrs. Slocomb petitioned then Governor O. William Coffin to have one flag be legally established as our state flag. Along with this request, she also submitted two designs for consideration.

In 1897, Mrs. Slocomb submitted a third flag design for consideration. The flag submitted was made of blue bunting twelve feet by eighteen feet. It had the state shield in white, bordered in silver and blue, and the old colonial seal of three clinging grapevines that were said to represent religion, liberty, and knowledge. Beneath the shield on a streamer was the state's motto "Qui, transtulet, sustinet," which translated means "He who hath transplanted, still sustains."

In August 1897, Mrs. Slocomb's design became Connecticut's official state flag. *(April 20, 2006)*

Connecticut flag designed by Mrs. Slocomb.
(Courtesy Jim Streeter)

# What's in a Name?

## Charles Q. Eldredge

A few months ago, I wrote about the once-popular Eldredge Museum on the Groton side of Mystic. Displaying a collection of over 7,000 curios items, this "one-man museum" was considered one of the most unique and interesting places to visit in southeastern Connecticut.

Mystic resident Charles Q. Eldredge, who founded and built the museum in 1917, provided his personal and unique collection of keepsakes, relics, souvenirs, and curios for the exhibit.

Born in Old Mystic in 1845, Eldredge was the last of eight children born to Christopher and Nancy Eldredge. For an unknown reason, none of the Eldredge siblings were provided with a middle initial in their names.

When Charles was four years old, he fell from the back of an ox cart and cut his forehead on a stone. Some have said it was this fall that affected his brain and accounted for his eccentric and almost bizarre behavior at times.

The story of the middle initial "Q" in Charles Eldredge's name has its beginning when he attended the Old Mystic School. The schoolhouse was a two-story building, with younger students attending classes downstairs. When students grew too tall to walk beneath a three-and-a-half-foot-high board attached to the wall, they "graduated" to the second floor. In those days, grades of classes were unheard-of, and only physical growth was used for a gauge of intelligence level.

A few years after moving to the upper level, the students learned that a new and very strict man had been hired as their teacher. The kids agreed amongst themselves to play a joke of sorts on the new teacher. When called upon by the teacher to provide their names, each would give a fictitious middle initial. Those who had a middle initial would change it, and those who did not would make one up. Eldredge was the first called upon to provide his name. When he responded, he added the middle initial "Q." This brought hearty laughs from all the other children, who subsequently reneged from the "name change" agreement. During subsequent roll calls throughout the remainder of the day, Eldredge would provide his newly found middle initial, and after doing so the entire class would respond with a large round of laughter. The teacher caught on very quickly, and the use of the fictitious middle initial brought a great deal of embarrassment and trouble to the young Eldredge. It seems that the teacher and school committee (now called the board of education) failed to see the humor in the act and felt that Eldredge had "committed a grievous offence against the morals and deportment of the school." Serious stuff back then! Eldredge was required to provide an apology to the teacher, school committee, and his classmates or else face expulsion from the school.

Charles provided the necessary apology and was forgiven for his act.

Although the middle initial "Q" was not part of the birth name given to Charles Eldredge, the initial "Q" became part of his legal name for the rest of his life. And, as a matter of fact, Eldredge provided one of his sons with the middle initial "Q."

We've all heard the saying "John Q. Citizen." This was the story of Groton's "Q" citizen. *(July 19, 2007)*

# Groton's Heroic Navy Divers

On May 23, 1939, the United States submarine *Squalus*, with fifty-six sailors and three civilians on board, sank in the waters off of Portsmouth, New Hampshire. The boat, which was built at the Portsmouth Navy Yard, was conducting a trial dive when a main induction value malfunctioned and caused flooding in the after compartments of the sub. Twenty-four sailors and two civilians drowned during this tragic occurrence. With the boat resting some 240 feet below the surface, thirty-three men remained alive in the sealed forward compartments.

Within a few hours after sinking, one of the greatest undersea rescue operations in history was organized to save the trapped crew. It was decided that a newly developed "rescue chamber" designed to save men from sunken submarines would be dispatched to remove the survivors. The Navy had five such chambers, and the one that was close enough to help the *Squalus* was aboard the USS *Falcon*, a submarine rescue ship home ported at the Submarine Base in Groton.

Interestingly, when the *Falcon* received the call to respond to the rescue, it was ill-prepared to do so. The boat was in the process of its annual overhaul, and its boilers were dead. The rescue chamber had been removed from the boat and most of the crew was on leave.

Within a few hours, in a phenomenal response to the emergency, the boilers were back in operation, the rescue chamber was reloaded, and, with the help of the police and Navy shore patrol, the remainder of the crew and divers had been rounded up and returned to the ship. The *Falcon* departed the sub base in the mid-afternoon and was moored over the *Squalus* early the next morning.

During the next twelve hours, the rescue chamber made four trips to and from the sunken boat and successfully rescued all thirty-three men.

Four divers assigned to the *Falcon*—William Badders, John Mihalowski, Orson L. Crandall, and James Harper McDonald—who participated in the rescue received the Medal of Honor for their heroic efforts.

The *Squalus* was subsequently raised and towed to the Portsmouth Navy Yard. She was decommissioned on November 15th of 1939. After being refitted, she was renamed the *Sailfish* and placed back in service in February 1940.

Groton can again be proud of having the Submarine Base and the men and women assigned there as part of its community. *(May 10, 2007)*

Medal of Honor winners, *left to right*,
Williams Badders, John Mihalowski, Orson Crandall, and James McDonald
(Courtesy Jim Streeter)

# Remembering a Groton Hero

## James E. Baker

Almost two years ago, I penned an article about the heroic efforts of several divers assigned to the USS *Falcon*, a submarine rescue ship home ported at the Groton Submarine Base. Those divers had risked their lives to rescue thirty-three men from the U.S. Submarine *Squalus* that sank off of Portsmouth, New Hampshire, on May 23, 1939.

In the article I recognized four divers who had participated in the rescue operation: William Badders, John Mihalowski, Orson. L. Crandall, and James Harper McDonald, who were subsequently awarded the Medal of Honor for their heroic efforts.

A few months after the article was published, a longtime Groton resident and personal friend, William Hart, who is also a highly decorated Korean War veteran, contacted me to say he was disappointed that the article had not mentioned the other thirty-nine divers who had taken part in the rescue operation and that they, too, had risked their lives to save the men on the *Squalus*. According to Mr. Hart, one of those divers was James E. Baker, a resident of Groton and a diving instructor at the Sub Base's diving tower. Mr. Baker had been awarded the Navy Cross, the highest medal that can be awarded by the Department of the Navy and the second highest award given for valor, for his heroic efforts during the *Squalus* operation.

According to research conducted by Mr. Hart and this author, Baker made numerous dives to the *Squalus* from the *Falcon*. As stated in the official transcript of the "Court of Inquiry" concerning the *Squalus*, one of the most dramatic dives performed during the *Squalus* rescue operation took place on May 25, 1939, when Baker attached the cable of the "Rescue Bell" to the torpedo hatch of the *Squalus*. The depth of this dive was 239 feet. No dive had been made before past the two-hundred-foot mark.

In late 2008, Mr. Hart provided me the detailed information he had garnered during his research. Shortly thereafter, upon reviewing the obituary write-up for James Baker, who died April 3, 1978, contact was made with the daughter of Mr. Baker, who was residing in New York. Coincidentally, it was discovered that the daughter, Carol, and this author had resided a few houses away from each other while growing up in Poquonnock Bridge, and we both recalled being acquainted with many of the same people and frequenting the same local "hangouts." Carol explained that her mother, Aurore Bonnenfant Baker, had prepared several scrapbook albums, which meticulously documented her husband's naval career. One of the albums contained a great deal of information about the *Squalus* diving operation.

A few weeks ago, Carol Baker paid this author a visit and brought along the albums, which I can only describe as "stupendous." I was so astonished at the amount of information and associated photographs contained in the albums relating the diving career of her father, that I suggested she should consider writing some type of memoir book.

Of particular interest in the album concerning Jim Baker's actions in the *Squalus* operation was the citation from the president of the United States awarding him the Navy Cross, which read:

> For extraordinary heroism in the line of his profession as a diver during the rescue and salvage operation following the sinking of the U.S.S. SQUALUS on 23 May 1930. His courage and devotion to duty in making repeated dangerous dives during the most difficult diving conditions characterizes conduct far above and beyond the call of duty.

After retiring from the Navy in 1945, Jim Baker became employed as a civil service worker in the Public Works Department at the Submarine Base. A quiet, efficient, and unassuming person, Jim rarely spoke about the courageous actions performed by the divers, including himself, during the *Squalus* rescue operation.

Jim subsequently became very active in community activities. He was a charter member of the Groton Lodge of Elks and served as the Lodge's steward from 1960 to 1968. He was also a life member of the Poquonnock Bridge Fire Department, Groton's Fleet Reserve, and the Charity and Relief Lodge of Masons in Mystic.

James Baker's actions in helping to save the thirty-three sailors on the *Squalus* were heroic, and Groton can be proud to say that he was then and continued until his death to be a resident of our community. As I have stated in previous articles, "You are not dead until you are forgotten." Mr. Baker is still alive in our thoughts.

As a note of interest, in early December of last year, Carl Bryson, another Groton resident and the last survivor rescued from the USS *Squalus*, passed away. He, too, will be sorely missed. William Hart and Carol Baker contributed to this article. *(March 26, 2009)*

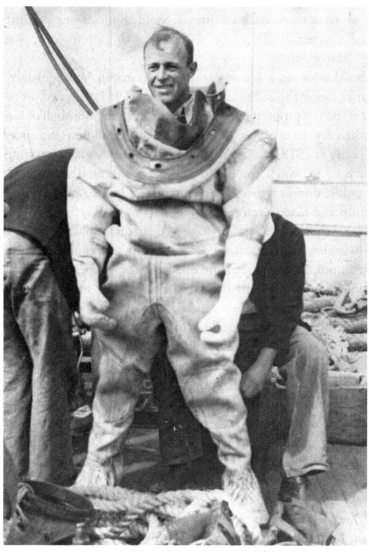

James E. Backer in his diving suit
(Courtesy Carol Baker)

# George Marquardt—A Community Leader

Beginning in 2004, Groton Utilities established the Jacqueline B. Nixon Community Service Award, recognizing a member of the community who has contributed his or her time, energy, and resources in making Groton a better place to work and live.

If we were to go back in time, I could think of one person who would be especially deserving of receiving this prestigious award—George Marquardt.

Mr. Marquardt, a lifelong resident of Groton, was probably best known as being the individual who, in late 1931, donated a twenty-five-acre tract of property on Meridian Street to the Borough of Groton (now the City) to establish a public park and a children's playground.

As early as 1919, Marquardt and his two sons began converting this property, which was a combination of farm pastureland, swampland, and a public dump, into a park of sorts. They graded over a portion of the dump and made a rough but suitable area to play baseball.

When the land was donated, Marquardt stipulated that it be called Washington Park, after President George Washington, and that a skating pond would be maintained on the property. Incidentally, the pond was subsequently named "Lake George" in memory of Mr. Marquardt after his death.

Today the park provides facilities for various sporting and recreational activities and is one of the best parks in southeastern Connecticut.

Now that we have discussed one of the major contributions Mr. Marquardt made to the community, we should discuss some of his other attributes and activities.

George Marquardt was educated at the local schools and for many years was connected with the firm called Marquardt Brothers, carpenters and builders. The Marquardts built many architecturally pleasing Victorian-style houses in the "Bank" area of Groton. They also established the Groton Lumber Company on Thames Street in the area where the Hell Cat Fishing Boat business is presently located. In later years the business was moved to Bridge Street and was subsequently sold. Many readers will recall it as the Diamond National Lumber Yard.

George Marquardt eventually ventured out on his own and operated a real estate business. He developed the land and built several houses on Morgan Court, off of Cottage Street, built five houses on Ramsdell Street in a place that was formerly a mud hole, and erected six double tenement houses on Granite Street in an area that had previously been deemed advisable to leave alone because of ledge.

In the early 1920s, after the first railroad bridge crossing the Thames River was converted into a motor vehicle bridge, Marquardt, who had a keen business sense, had the foresight to purchase property close to the highway near the exit on the Groton side of the bridge. He then built the Bridge Plaza Gas Station, a large gasoline and service station, which attracted a great deal of business from vehicles traveling both ways over the bridge. The station was equipped with nine separate gasoline pumps and retailed every popular brand of gasoline and oil. The Plaza also housed a motorcar "taxi" business, a small luncheonette, and a tobacco store. Mr. Marquardt also maintained an office for his real estate business in the building.

Mr. Marquardt served as a member of the Borough's Board of Wardens and Burgesses for twenty years, and at the time of his death in 1932, he was the senior warden. While a warden, he served on the finance committee and devoted much of his time ensuring improvements to sidewalks and roads. He was known as "the father of the sidewalk movement in the Borough."

Besides his business and government activities, Mr. Marquardt was a charter member of the Fairview Lodge of the Independent Order of Odd Fellows and the Groton Lions Club. He was a charter member of the Pioneer Hose Fire Company. He was an active member of the Groton Congregational Church.

As you can see from this brief biographical narrative, George Marquardt was an extremely active person who contributed a great deal to Groton. Although he will not be a recipient of the Groton Utilities Jacqueline B. Nixon Community Service award, at least by this article he will be recognized for providing much to Groton's history. *(November 8, 2007)*

Bridge Plaza Filling Station (late 1920s)
(Courtesy John Scott)

# William Eugene Seely

Two years ago, the electors of Groton approved funding to build two new elementary schools. Subsequent to the vote, the author of this article had the distinct pleasure of being a member of a committee who proposed that one of the schools be named after longtime Groton resident and community volunteer Katherine Kolnaski.

This is not the first time a Groton school has been named to honor special residents or community volunteers. One such special resident for whom a school has been named is William Eugene Seely.

Mr. Seely was the first Groton resident who gave his life in World War II. He was in the U.S. Navy and was stationed on the USS *Arizona*. He was killed when the Japanese bombed Pearl Harbor on December 7, 1941. This week marks the sixty-fourth anniversary of the bombing.

In 1954, the newly constructed elementary school located near the Navy housing in the western section of the town was christened the William Seely Elementary School.

A familiar phrase used by many Vietnam War veterans as well as by the family members and friends of men and women who have been killed or lost in action in the wars and conflicts in which they served is "A man is not dead until he is forgotten."

It is thus fitting that we remember William Seely. He was born on October 8, 1922. He attended Pleasant Valley Elementary School and graduated from Robert E. Fitch High School in 1940. He enlisted in the United States Navy on his eighteenth birthday in 1940. He was just nineteen when he gave his life for his country.

Longtime Groton resident Art Greenleaf, who graduated from Fitch High School with William Seely, remembers him as being a quiet youth who worked as a clerk after school hours at the small Aben Hardware store on Thames Street. They also attended Sunday school together at the Groton Heights Baptist Church.

Well, Mr. Seely, you are not forgotten, and I, for one, would like to thank you for what you have given to our country. *(December 9, 2005)*

William E. Seely
(Courtesy Town of Groton Board of Education)

# "Top Guns" from Groton

It wasn't too many years ago when the City of Groton (formerly the Borough of Groton) Police Department fielded a "pistol team" that was considered one of the best in New England.

In the early 1950s, police officers throughout the country held the distinct and unfortunate reputation of being "the worst shots in the world" when it came to the weapons they were carrying. The Federal Bureau of Investigation instituted firearms training programs for police officers from local municipalities and also provided police departments with firearms training so as to improve their shooting abilities.

Two young police officers from Groton, Marty Artale and Joe Sandora, decided to take advantage of the training. They ultimately graduated from the FBI's Firearms Instructor School and began training many of their fellow officers on the Borough and Town of Groton Police Departments.

In the beginning, the officers practiced shooting at a makeshift range in the wooded area on the Groton Utilities filtration plant property in Poquonnock. Their homemade range consisted of a large three-foot piece of steel (donated by the Electric Boat Company), propped up at an angle against a tree, with a paper target attached. Although they carried .38-caliber guns on duty, they used small .22-caliber bullets when they practiced at their range.

Artale and Sandora, who would practice at least once or twice a week, became expert shots and decided to organize a pistol league, where they could shoot in competition with other shooters from various organizations and clubs in New London County.

In the winter of 1953 and 1954, with the help of Bill Genth, a retired Navy chief, and Bud Farrar from the New London *Day* newspaper, they officially organized what became known as the New London County Pistol League. Interest in the league grew rapidly and before too long teams from the Coast Guard Academy, the Submarine Base Marines, Pfizer, Electric Boat Company, the Naval Underwater Sound Lab, Mystic Rod & Gun Club, Quaker Hill, and of course the Borough of Groton participated in weekly shooting matches.

Many of the matches were held at shooting ranges at the Coast

Guard Academy, the former railroad police building on Water Street in New London, and the New London Armory.

In the early 1960s, the City of Groton Police Department organized a pistol team to participate in "police combat" pistol matches that were held throughout New England. Besides Artale and Sandora, core members of the team included Jim Sheehan, Ben Gillis, Frank Bailey, Jack Edwards, Bill Meisel, Jack Dunn, Bob Walters, Larry Gerrish, and Jim Streeter. The group's competition included teams from New York City, Providence, Philadelphia, and Boston. Needless to say, the competition was keen.

By the mid-1960s, the police department had built a modern "police combat" shooting range at the Filtration Plant, and members of the team were constantly using these facilities to better their shooting skills. The City's police team became well respected throughout New England and won more than its fair share of individual and team trophies and medals. Artale, Sandora, and Sheehan became "Master Shots," which required consistently shooting a score of over 280 out of 300. In a police combat match held in Hartford in August of 1966, Artale shot a perfect score to take first place in a field of sixty-five.

Over the years, interest in shooting competitively subsided, and by the mid-'70s the team had disbanded. Marty Artale contributed to this article. *(October 18, 2007)*

# Medal of Honor Recipient


# Robert A. Gray


The Congressional Medal of Honor is the highest military award in the United States. The medal was first awarded in the Civil War by the president of the United States to a recipient whose voluntary action was above and beyond the call of duty and at the risk of one's own life. Of the tens of millions of men and women who have served the United States in times of need since the Civil War, only 3,456 have received the Medal of Honor.

Robert A. Gray, a twenty-seven-year-old stonemason from Groton, was a recipient of this prestigious award during the Civil War.

Mr. Gray was born in 1834 in Philadelphia, Pennsylvania, and enlisted in Company C of the Twenty-first Connecticut Infantry in August of 1862. He was promoted to sergeant in December 1862. Sergeant Gray was awarded the Medal of Honor as a result of his courageous and brave actions during a contested battle of Drewry's Bluff, Virginia, on May 16, 1864, in which he risked his life while retrieving a wounded soldier during the heat of battle. Although fellow soldiers had warned him not to risk his life to save the downed soldier, Sergeant Gray's response was "I will try if I lose my life." Fellow soldiers who had witnessed the heroic event stated it was a miracle that Sergeant Gray had survived as "shot and shell were falling like a shower of rice."

After the war, Mr. Gray returned to Groton, where he spent the rest of his life. He resided on Ramsdell Street in Groton Bank and became a partner in the Groton-based granite and marble quarry business named Merritt, Gray & Company. He took an active interest in community civic life, serving as a representative to the General Assembly in 1880–81 and as vice president of the Groton Heights Centennial Committee in 1881. He was an active worker and participant in all steps for the perpetuation of historic Fort Griswold and served as vice president of the Groton Heights Centennial Committee in 1881.

Robert A. Gray
(Courtesy National Archives)

Sergeant Gray passed away on November 22, 1906, and is buried in the Colonel Ledyard Cemetery, where, ironically, he had worked for over ten years cutting grass, removing and burying stumps, and building walls.

In his last will and testament, he directed that a memorial, dedicated to all of the men in Groton who served in the Civil War, be provided to the Groton Monument Association.

On July 4, 1916, at a ceremony attended by approximately two hundred people, the monument was dedicated and named the "Robert A. Gray Monument." It is located in the Fort Griswold State Park near the Monument House Museum.

It is with great honor we can say that a true hero of our country was a resident of Groton. *(May 27, 2005)*

# Groton and *"The New England Almanac"*

## Nathan Daball

During the Columbus Day weekend, while spending a few days at our family's vacation home in Groton, Vermont—*yes, Groton*—my wife and I had the opportunity to go to an outdoor antique show. As usual, while my wife was browsing the antique furniture, jewelry, and paintings, I engaged in my favorite activity of rummaging through boxes of ephemera (a fancy word for paper advertisements, newspapers, magazines, postcards, books, etc.) in hopes of finding a historical treasure to add to my own collection.

Well, as luck would have it, I discovered a small cigar box containing a stack of seventeen small booklets titled *The New England Almanac and Farmer's Friend*, bearing dates ranging from 1854 to 1880. I immediately recognized the books as having been produced by the Daboll family of Centre Groton, Connecticut. Although I knew I had several of the Daboll almanacs at home, I could not pass them up and took the chance that they would not be duplicates to those I already had. The going price of the Daboll almanacs is generally $5 to $25 each, so needless to say, I was quite pleased when I walked away with the entire pile for $12.

In the early days, *The New England Almanac and Farmer's Friend* was one of the most popular and widely read publications throughout New England. Having a copy of the annually published almanac was a "must" for anyone involved in fishing, agriculture, or other outdoor activities. Information printed in these almanacs included timetables for the waxing and waning cycles of the moon, high-water tide tables, and a complete daily listing of the sun's and moon's rising and setting times. The booklet contained daily "judgments of the weather"— predictions that were relied upon by many of its readers. Also contained in these booklets was information relating to special events, festivals, and other remarkable dates; postal rates; locations of courts; lists of lighthouses in Long Island Sound; and lists of ships involved in the fishing of whales. Another section in the booklet, titled "Miscellaneous," provided political commentary, poetry, and other tidbits of historical and statistical information. Information such as the following, which appeared in the 1871 edition, catches one's attention: "Among 10,00 persons, one arrives at the age of 100 years, one in 500 the age of 90, and one in 100 lives to the age of 60."

The almanac or astronomical-type diary in Connecticut can be traced back to about 1750, when it was published in the *Connecticut Gazette* by T. Green and Sons of New London.

In 1773, [Master] Nathan Daboll, of Groton, a self-taught and distinguished mathematician—subject matter for a future article—began a series of almanacs titled *Daboll's New England Almanac*, which was also published by T. Green and Sons. A few years before his death in 1818, Nathan became blind, and his son, Nathan, known as "the Squire," took over compiling the almanac. As a note of interest, Squire Nathan was a member of the Connecticut House of Representatives and State Senate in the 1830s and was also a judge of probate. He renamed the almanac the *New England Almanac and Farmers Friend* and continued compiling it until his death in 1863, at which time his son, David A., took over the responsibilities. In 1897, David Austin, the great-grandson of Master Nathan, assumed the duties from his father, David A.

Subsequently members of the Daboll family who continued preparing the almanac in the nineteenth century were Loren and Ernest. After the death of Ernest Daboll in 1967, no other family members were willing to carry on the business. The almanac was sold to the *Yankee Magazine* and [Daboll] *New England Almanac*, which had been published for over 195 years, passed into history.

Incidentally, I gathered up my collection of the Daboll almanacs and found that, with the seventeen purchased in Vermont, I now have over ninety, the earliest being 1797 and the latest being 1906. While conducting the research for this article, I consumed a considerable amount of time browsing through them—needless to say, they are interesting reading.

Did I mention that the Daboll homestead house, where Master Daboll produced his almanac, still stands on Candlewood Road in Center Groton? *(October 30, 2008)*

NUMBER ONE HUNDRED AND THIRTY-ONE.

# THE NEW ENGLAND

# ALMANAC

## AND FARMERS' FRIEND.

FOR THE YEAR OF OUR LORD CHRIST

# 1903:

BEING THE SEVENTH AFTER BISSEXTILE OR LEAP YEAR,

—AND THE—

One Hundred and Twenty-Seventh of American Independence.

Calculated for the Meridian of New London, Latitude 41° 21' N., Longitude 72° 05' W.

## BY DAVID A. DABOLL,

CENTER GROTON, CONN.

Containing besides the Astronomical Calculations, a Variety of Matter both Useful and Entertaining.

THE HUSBANDMAN.

" Time is a wise, consistent husbandman;
For first he sows the fruitfullness of smiles
Upon our faces, youths' soft dewy tears
And early sunshine. Then he brings his plow
And drives his wand'ring furrows ruthlessly,
Sows cares and disciplines; and last of all,
When life's experience is golden ripe,
He swings betimes his gentle, painless scythe
Amid the bearded harvest bent with snow."

NEW LONDON :

PUBLISHED AND SOLD BY L. E. DABOLL, 94 STATE STREET.

(Price 8 cents, postpaid 10 cents.)

NEW LONDON PRINTING CO., NEW LONDON, CONN.

1903 edition of the Daboll's
*New England Almanac and Farmer's Friend*
(Courtesy Jim Streeter)

# Chapter 4

## Events and Happenings

# Goodyear Blimp's First Visit to Groton

A few weeks ago, while at work in Meriden, a friend and co-worker, whose family had resided for years in the Bakers Cove area of Groton, mentioned to me that she had recently come into possession of her late aunt's diary containing handwritten entries from the mid-1930s.

While reading the entries, she came across one that piqued her curiosity. On October 8th, 1935, her aunt had written: "Tuesday Night—While home eating supper a Goodyear dirigible landed on field at airport." No further mention was made in the diary about the subject. My friend wanted to know if I could determine what the occasion was that warranted the visit of the Goodyear airship.

A story appearing in the *Day* newspaper on October 9, 1935, relayed some interesting facts about the airship's visit.

Evidently, while en route from New York to Providence, the crew discovered repairs were needed to a generator on the ship that operated large neon electric advertising signs located on the sides of the craft.

The landing was a surprise to airport personnel, as no notification was received that the dirigible would be landing. Upon arrival in the area of the airport, the ship circled the field for some time. While hovering over the airfield, a crew member on the blimp was heard yelling down that they were waiting for a ground crew before they would land. The ground crew was believed to be coming from New York.

The running lights and the engine noise from the blimp could be seen and heard for quite some distance. The ship's presence and the fact that it was making several circles around the field brought a great deal of attention. Before too long, all of the roads leading to the airport were jammed with cars, and a crowd of people, estimated to be in excess of five hundred, "swarmed" to the airport field to view the blimp and to watch it land. Traffic congestion was so bad that a state trooper was sent to handle crowds and to direct traffic.

The blimp landed at about 7:30 PM and remained for only about thirty minutes while the necessary repairs to the generator were made. Then, without any fanfare, the famous Goodyear blimp departed the area.

Further research revealed that Goodyear had a fleet of blimps at the time, and it is believed that the one that landed at Groton was, in all probability, named the *Defender*. Built in late 1929 in Wingfoot Lake near Akron, Ohio, it was launched by the famous aviator Amelia Earhart and was the first airship to carry a lighted sign. Called "Neon-O-Gram," ten removable aluminum framed panels were attached to the side of the ship, allowing a static text to be displayed with neon light tubes. Each panel measured six feet tall and four feet wide and weighed thirty-five pounds.

The *Defender* was subsequently purchased by the Navy and designated the *G-1*. She was lost in a midair collision with another airship on June 8, 1942, and twelve people died in the crash.

I still recall, while growing up in Poquonnock Bridge in the 1950s, seeing many Navy blimps traveling over our house. Those memories will remain forever. The 1935 visit of the Goodyear blimp at the Groton airfield certainly deserves an entry in anyone's diary, and I hope this article will bring recall to such a memorable event. *(December 13, 2007)*

# The Great Hurricane of 1938

## Part I

September 21st will mark the seventieth anniversary of one of the most powerful and destructive storms ever to strike New England. It killed almost seven hundred people and caused damage estimated at over $306 million, which, by today's standards, equates to almost $17 billion. The storm is said to be the worst natural disaster to have struck Connecticut during the twentieth century, and it certainly did not spare Groton.

The hurricane pretty much came without warning, and most residents were unaware of the oncoming onslaught. Unlike today, there were no satellites, radar, or even hurricane hunter aircraft to track such storms to provide advance warning. Based upon reports from ships along the Eastern Seaboard, weather forecasters believed that this particular storm would remain offshore and would not be a threat to New England. The weather forecast published in the *Day* newspaper the day before the storm called for "rain and cooler temperatures with moderate shifting winds becoming north or northeast" for the day the storm struck.

There were other reasons the storm took many by surprise. The technology then was not what it is today. Communication was mostly by radio—there were no televisions, no cable, and no computers. Yes, there were telephones; however, the advancing winds of the hurricane caused numerous telephone and electric lines to come down. Radio stations and newspapers were unable to provide warnings because the storm was moving so rapidly up the coast. Many believed that the storm was just a strong "nor'easter" associated with the heavy rains that had fallen across Connecticut for the preceding four days. The last hurricane to strike New England was in September of 1815, and there was no one living who recalled it. Many thus believed that a hurricane would never hit the area.

Once it was determined that the hurricane had turned to the west

77

and was indeed going to strike the East Coast, it was too late.

The winds from the hurricane began in the late morning and the full force of the storm struck Groton at about 3:00 PM. Classified as a Category 3 hurricane, it moved at a speed of approximately seventy miles per hour. Sustained winds of ninety miles per hour and gusts reaching over one hundred twenty miles per hour were experienced during the peak of the storm. The Weather Bureau estimated the size of the hurricane to be approximately five hundred miles wide with an eye as much as fifty miles wide. A barometric pressure chart for the area on the day of the storm recorded the pressure at about 28.8 inches at the peak of the storm.

The heavy rains that were mentioned earlier would ultimately contribute to the extreme damage experienced throughout the area. The water from these rains, estimated to be about ten inches, on top of the three to six inches of rain accompanying the hurricane, contributed to the severe flooding that took place throughout New London County.

Adding to the destruction and devastation caused by the storm was the fact that it struck at the peak of high tide. The tides had been expected to be higher than usual before the storm because of the autumnal equinox (when the sun and moon are both in line with the Earth, causing a double gravitation pull); but with the surge caused by the storm, the tides were over seventeen feet above normal levels. Waves between thirty and fifty feet high pounded the coastline with millions of tons of seawater. The impact of the storm surge was so strong that it was recorded on the earthquake seismograph at Fordham University in New York City.

The combination of the winds, floods, storm surge, and waves not only wiped out thousands of homes and hundreds of thousands of trees, but also caused extensive damage to bridges, utilities, and rail lines. Many of the lives that were lost as a result of the storm occurred when individuals came out of their homes when the winds calmed and the sun came out to take a look at the damage. Little did they realize that this was the eye of the hurricane, and within a short period of time, they were caught in the backlash of this powerful storm.

Incidentally, the naming of tropical storms and hurricanes began in 1953. Although the hurricane of 1938 does not have an official name, it was nicknamed "The Long Island Express." Today a rotating list of male and female names is used over a six-year cycle in naming the storms. A name is retired from the list if the storm was deadly or costly.

The destruction of property in Groton was enormous. Next week's article will contain descriptions of the damage and also relay some stories by individuals who experienced the storm. *(September 4, 2008)*

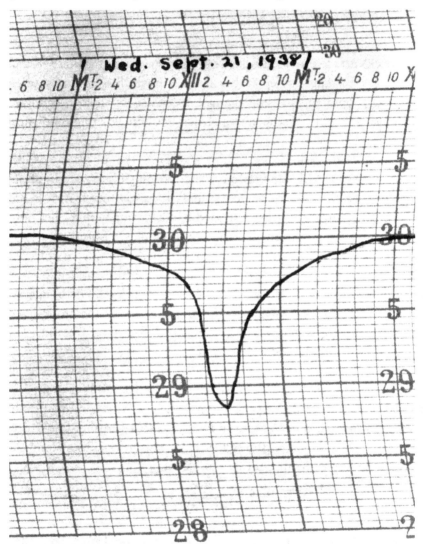

Barometric chart reading during the Hurricane of 1938
(Courtesy Mystic River Historical Society)

# The Great Hurricane of 1938

# Part II

Last week's article provided a description of the hurricane of 1938 that struck New England on September 21st, taking the lives of almost seven hundred people and causing damage estimated at today's standards at almost $17 billion. The storm struck without warning, and most residents were unaware of its impending onslaught.

Nicknamed "The Long Island Express," the outskirts of the hurricane began to hit the area in the late-morning hours, and by about 3:00 PM, Groton was experiencing the full force of the storm. It was a Category 3 hurricane with sustained winds of ninety miles per hour and gusts reaching over one hundred twenty miles per hour.

Heavy rains, in total over ten inches, had plummeted into the area for four days prior to the hurricane, and the storm added another six inches. The accumulation of this rain caused flooding throughout New London County. When the heavy winds struck, the ground was so saturated with water that an estimated 275 million trees in New England were uprooted and destroyed.

The storm struck during the peak of high tide, and the water levels of the tide exceeded seventeen feet above normal. With the surge of the tide came waves thirty to fifty feet in height. This combination of the winds, floods, storm surge, and waves resulted in the destruction of thousands of homes, businesses, and recreational facilities along the coast, including those in Groton and New London.

A total of ten storm-related deaths, many as a result of drowning, were reported in Groton and Mystic. Two of the deaths were the captain and a crew member of a thirty-five-foot cabin cruiser from Oyster Bay, Long Island, which crashed on the shore of the Plant estate at Avery Point.

It was said that every house of worship in Mystic was damaged by the wind and flying debris. The strong winds caused the Methodist Church on Willow Street to completely collapse. The steeple and clock tower of the Union Baptist Church was blown off of the building, and the steeple of the Congregational Church also toppled. St. Patrick's Catholic Church sustained major water damage after winds caused a chimney to fall through the roof, creating a large hole.

Almost every summer cottage at Bluff Point was destroyed by the storm. Many of the summer homes and cottages at Groton Long Point and Eastern Point sustained extensive wind and water damage, and several were blown off of their foundations. The large community center "Casino" at Groton Long Point was destroyed when it was blown off of its foundation, and all of the bathhouses and cabanas at the Shennecossett Beach Club were completely washed away.

The fleet at the Shennecossett Yacht Club was almost a total loss, as were the buildings and wharves. Groton resident Tom Migliaccio, who was working at the Yacht Club when the storm struck, recalls the difficulty he and fellow workers had as they tried to secure several of the boats that were still in the water. While trying to maneuver one boat, which had its engine running, he was knocked overboard. After falling into the water, the wind and waves caused the boat to pass over him several times before he was able to get to safety. Fortunately he was not struck by the prop of the still-running engine. Migliaccio stated that the storm became so intense that he and the other workers sought refuge in a concrete garage on the Plant property next to the club.

The hurricane wrecked many of the businesses and homes on the Groton bank of the Thames River. The places worst struck were the ferry slip, the buildings, wharves, and docks for the Spicer Ice & Coal and G. M. Long [fish] Companies, and many buildings and homes along Thames Street.

Damage was so extensive that Martial Law was declared in New London County, and members of the State's Army National Guard patrolled the streets. Special passes were issued by the State Police to permit food deliveries and to allow individuals owning homes along the coast to recover personal belongings.

In conducting research for this article, I found it ironic that within a few days of the storm, several local insurance agencies had placed advertisements in the newspaper encouraging home owners and businesses to purchase hurricane and windstorm protection insurance. I don't think you would see such advertisements today, and I am sure the rates would be astronomical.

The Great Hurricane of 1938 was indeed the worst natural disaster to have struck Connecticut during the twentieth century. The death and destruction caused by the storm will always be imbedded in the history of our community. Although there have been many books written about the hurricane and its effect on New England, there has never been a book written about its impact on Groton and Mystic. There is certainly sufficient material to do so, and hopefully someday, someone will find the time to do so. *(September 11, 2008)*

"Fats" Aitkens, *left*, and "Slim" Bailey of Groton patrol Eastern Point after Martial Law was declared after the Hurricane of 1938. (Courtesy Tom Migliaccio)

# A Visit to Groton by First Lady Jacqueline Kennedy

Over the years, many dignitaries, including several presidents and first ladies of the United States, have paid visits to Groton to participate in keel-laying and launch ceremonies for submarines at the Electric Boat Division's shipyard. One of the most memorable visits took place on May 8, 1962, when Jacqueline Lee Bouvier Kennedy, wife of President John F. Kennedy, christened the ballistic missile submarine USS *Lafayette* (*SSBN-616*).

Although the weather on that day was overcast and cold, an estimated nine thousand workers and three thousand invited guests witnessed the launch ceremony. Hundreds of others were present at the Groton–New London Airport to greet Mrs. Kennedy after her plane landed. Others lined the roads leading from the Groton–New London Airport to the shipyard, and along Eastern Point Road, to catch a glimpse of America's beautiful First Lady.

Albert Hartunian, who operated a laundry business on Poquonnock Road, displayed two special American flags, one having thirty-six stars and the other with forty-six stars, in the front of his store in hopes of catching Mrs. Kennedy's attention. Unfortunately, when the limousine carrying her passed, her head was turned the other way to wave at children from the Sacred Heart School, who were given a recess and stood on Poquonnock Road to wave at Mrs. Kennedy when her cavalcade rode by.

Everest Brustolon, a worker at the shipyard, on the other hand, was one of the fortunate ones. As the presidential limo traveled down the shipyard's main yard hill, he enthusiastically welcomed Mrs. Kennedy with waves and was rewarded when she looked at him and waved back.

Security for the visit was extensive. Every member of the Borough of Groton's Police Department was on duty patrolling the streets and keeping about one hundred "peace protestors" in check outside the shipyard's main gate. A contingent of eight Secret Service agents, a dozen state troopers, and members of EB's security staff kept a careful eye on all visitors inside the yard to ensure the safety of the First Lady.

A report of a man with a rifle in a car a few streets away from the shipyard caused a stir. Borough Police Sergeant Marty Artale quickly located and stopped the vehicle. It was ascertained that the young man operating the vehicle, who had a .22-caliber single-shot rifle in the backseat, was on his way to go hunting for squirrels. After a thorough "going over" the man was permitted to go.

An after-launch party for about eight hundred special guests of the launching was held at the elegant and luxurious Griswold Hotel at Eastern Point. As the story goes, Electric Boat had lavishly refurbished a four-room suite at the hotel where Mrs. Kennedy rested for about three-quarters of an hour. The cost to rebuild the suite was said to be $10,000. Outrageously expensive, if you ask me, for such a short period of time, even at today's prices.

An interesting and uncanny piece of information recently surfaced concerning Mrs. Kennedy's visit to the Griswold Hotel. It seems that although strict security precautions were in place to protect the First Lady, one area was completely overlooked. A group of five young boys from the Eastern Point area, who were thoroughly familiar with ways of "sneaking" into the hotel, found their way to a location beneath the front entrance stairs where they caught a close-up glimpse of the First Lady as she arrived and entered the building. By the way, I promised the source of this information that I would consider it privileged communications and that his name would remain anonymous.

For those golf enthusiasts who play at the Shennecossett Golf Course—the next time you tee-off on the eighteenth hole, you will be standing in the area where the president's Marine helicopter landed to pick up Mrs. Kennedy when she departed Groton.

There are so many interesting stories and tidbits of information about Mrs. Kennedy's short stay in Groton that one could probably write a short book about it. Indeed, it was an honor and a privilege to have had First Lady Jacqueline Kennedy come to Groton, and her visit will certainly be remembered by many as an important and memorial time in Groton's history. *(April 10, 2008)*

# Groton's "Rum Running" Scandal

## Part I

During the period of 1920 through 1933, the sale, manufacture, and transportation transportation of alcohol was constitutionally banned throughout the United States. This period of time in our country's history was called the Prohibition era.

Prohibition laws did not include the "simple" possession or consumption of the spirits, as it was assumed that if the supply was "cut off," a drastic reduction in its demand and consumption would follow. Unfortunately, this was not the case and the demand for liquor increased.

Although illegal in the United States, surrounding countries, including Canada, Mexico, and the Caribbean, had distilleries and breweries that could contribute to fulfilling the demand caused by Prohibition. Illegal breweries within the United States also entered the supply market.

Smuggling of illegal spirits into and around the country became big business, as the profits were enormous. Transporting illegal alcohol over land was called "bootlegging" and bringing it in by water was referred to as "Rum Running."

One major social problem that is attributed to these illegal smuggling activities was the involvement of organized crime and associated racketeering activities, including corrupting law enforcement agencies.

Unfortunately, southeastern Connecticut was not immune to such illegal activities, and in March of 1931, one of the largest scandals involving corruption within a law enforcement agency happened in Groton.

Although the incident occurred over seventy-five years ago, to avoid any embarrassment to family members, the real names of those involved will not be used in this article.

During Prohibition, ships carrying large cargos of alcohol would anchor in international waters off the coast of New York, Rhode Island, and Connecticut, in an area called "Rum Row," where they would await the arrival of smaller boats contracted by organized crime members and other interested parties to make smuggling runs to predesignated "drop-off points" on land. The Coast Guard had numerous crafts that would patrol the offshore waters of these states to intercept the "Rum Running" craft. Many of the Coast Guard boats involved in the "Rum Running" interdiction activities were moored at the State Pier in New London.

In the early-morning hours of March 16, 1931, the Coast Guard observed a small speedboat, laden with sacks of liquor, chugging along in the waters in Long Island Sound, and obviously heading for an undisclosed harbor on the north side of Long Island. The Guard immediately pursued the boat and, in doing so, fired several shots across the boat's bow. The boat and its cargo were ultimately seized.

A short while later, at a little after 2:30 AM, another speedboat was observed traveling through the waters near Race Rock Lighthouse heading toward the Connecticut shore. The Guard gave chase and, in an attempt to stop the boat, found it necessary to fire several warning shots at this vessel. The boat continued to pull away from the Coast Guard boat, and, because of its speed, it was felt that the boat was in all probability not carrying any contraband and was possibly a decoy to draw attention away from other "rum runners" working the area. The pursuit was thus aborted.

While all this was taking place, a crowd of about fifty men, with trucks and automobiles, was gathered in the vicinity of the old Griswold Hotel wharf at Groton's Eastern Point. The gathering raised little to no suspicion for several reasons: (1) the time of the day, (2) the fact the hotel was closed for the season, and (3) the houses in and around the hotel's location were only occupied during the summer months. It was obvious that the purpose of the gathering was to engage in the receipt and subsequent transportation and distribution of illegal alcohol. Using the Griswold Hotel dock for these illegal activities was especially brazen in consideration of the fact that Coast Guard boats passed this point traveling to and from the State Pier.

In the meantime, a Borough of Groton police patrolman, who we will identify as Officer *Peters*, while on night patrol in the business section of the borough, entered a garage where he overhead a telephone conversation detailing information about arranging for two trucks to pick up a delivery of illegal alcohol at the Griswold wharf. Officer *Peters* immediately went into action. To be continued next week. *(November 15, 2007)*

# Groton's "Rum Running" Scandal

# Part II

In the early morning hours of March 16, 1931, a group of about fifty men, two trucks, and several cars gathered in the area of the Griswold Hotel wharf in Groton in anticipation of receiving a load of illegal alcohol that was expected to be delivered via a "Rum Running" boat from a "mother ship" anchored in international waters off the coast of Connecticut and New York.

Little would it be known that this one activity would result in what was considered one of the largest scandals involving corruption in a police agency in southeastern Connecticut. Although the incident occurred over seventy-five years ago, to avoid any embarrassment to family members, the real names of those involved will not be used in this article.

While the men awaited their delivery, a Borough of Groton policeman, *Pete Peters*, was on night patrol in the business section of the borough and, after entering a local garage, overhead a telephone conversation detailing information about two trucks destined to pick up a delivery of illegal alcohol at the Griswold Hotel wharf.

Officer *Peters* left the garage and promptly located Patrolmen *Ed Jones* and *Tom Wills* and advised them of the conversation he had just overheard. All three then drove to Eastern Point and parked their car in the area of the Shennecossett Country Club. The officers then walked across the golf links and down to the rear of the Griswold Hotel, where they were joined by Officer *Bill Snow*, who was on patrol duty in the area. The four officers then scouted about and observed the gathering of about fifty men, two trucks, and about a dozen cars in the vicinity of the hotel's wharf. The "bad guys" had lookouts posted at various points; however, the officers were not spotted.

Believing they were outnumbered, the officers decided to call the Connecticut State Police barracks in Groton, which at the time was located on Thames Street near Bridge Street, and asked that troopers be sent to the area to assist in making arrests.

The State Police sergeant on duty immediately dispatched ten troopers to respond to the area. Officer *Jones* then left the hotel area and went up to Eastern Point Road, where he was to meet the trooper so they could conduct a stealthy approach on the gang involved in the smuggling activities.

Meanwhile, the Coast Guard patrol boats continued to pursue and fire shots over the bows of boats suspected as being "Rum Runners" destined to smuggle their booties of alcohol to drop-off points on the coasts of Rhode Island, New York, and Connecticut.

While the State Police was en route to the Griswold, the men and vehicles at the wharf suddenly scrambled and deserted the area before any "Rum Running" vessel arrived. It was suspected that the gang had overheard the shots being fired by the Coast Guard and felt it was best to clear the area to avoid arrest.

The state troopers encountered and stopped the trucks on Eastern Point Road. Although nothing was found to warrant detaining the trucks or passengers, the individuals were well-known as having previously engaged in illegal alcohol-smuggling activities.

The following morning, rumors were rampant that several Groton police officers and other prominent Borough officials had received bribes to permit illegal smuggling of alcohol. The bribery allegations were that Patrolmen *Peters, Jones,* and *Wills* had accepted money to permit the landing of the illegal liquor at the Griswold boat wharf and that Police Captain *Tony Webb* had also received a bribe to keep his men from "seeing too much." One has to remember that, at the time, the police captain was the highest-ranking official in the department.

Borough of Groton Police Commissioners *John Hardy* and *Jim Brooks*, who had heard that they had also been implicated in the bribe allegations, began their own internal investigation into the police activities. Within twenty-four hours, the commissioners developed sufficient information that would clear the accusation made against them, but would in turn bring embarrassment to the Borough and more specifically its police department.

The underlying truth about bribes, as well as the suspicious and almost unethical behavior by several Borough police officers, can almost be described as coming out of a script for a comical satire. The details about these activities will be discussed in next week's article. *(November 22, 2007)*

The wharf at the Griswold Hotel in the 1930s
(Courtesy Jim Streeter)

# Groton's "Rum-Running" Scandal

# The Conclusion

This is the concluding part of the series detailing the illegal alcohol smuggling incident that took place in Groton in March of 1931, involving the taking of bribes by police officers in Groton. Although the incident happened over seventy-five years ago, to avoid embarrassment to family members, the names of those involved have been changed.

In the early-morning hours of March 16, 1931, during the Prohibition era, a group of about fifty men waited with their vehicles at the wharf at Groton's Griswold Hotel for the arrival of a "Rum Running" boat to make a delivery of illegal alcohol.

While the men awaited their delivery, *Pete Peters*, a Borough of Groton policeman, while making rounds at a garage in the business section of the Borough, overheard a conversation about the anticipated delivery at the hotel.

*Peters*, along with Patrolmen *Ed Jones* and *Tom Wills*, drove to the area and parked a short distance from the hotel. They walked, undetected, to the rear of the hotel and were joined by Officer *Bill Snow*, who was on duty in the area. The officers scouted the area and, after observing the large gathering of men, decided to contact the State Police to ask for assistance in making arrests.

While awaiting the arrival of state troopers, the men and vehicles at the wharf suddenly scrambled and deserted the area. State troopers en route to the hotel encountered and stopped several of the vehicles on Eastern Point Road. No contraband was found, and the individuals in the vehicles were not detained.

The following morning, as the story of the aborted delivery at the Griswold surfaced, rumors were rampant that several Borough policemen, including *Peters, Jones,* and *Wills,* as well as other prominent Borough officials, including the police commissioners, had accepted bribes to permit the smuggling of alcohol. It was also rumored that Police Captain *Tony Webb*, the highest-ranking officer in the department, had received money to have his men "turn a blind side" to the activities.

Without any consideration of impropriety or improper action, Borough Police Commissioners *John Hardy* and *Jim Brooks* began their own inquiry into the matter. Within twenty-four hours, they had developed sufficient information to clear the allegations against themselves; however, their probe had turned up evidence to substantiate some of the other allegations.

Captain *Webb* admitted he had received a "tip" about the scheduled delivery at the hotel's wharf and that he had directed Officer *Snow*, who was to be on duty in the area, "not to see too much and to stay in his office [near the hotel]." It was subsequently learned that *Webb* had received $100 to "let it [the delivery] go."

Upon the recommendation of the Commissioners *Hardy* and *Brooks*, Captain *Webb* was demoted to patrolman and suspended from the department, without pay, for thirty days. Officer *Snow* was found to be guilty of conduct unbecoming an officer and received a thirty-day suspension, without pay.

Meanwhile, the allegations against *Peters, Jones,* and *Wills* took a strange twist. All three admitted to accepting money from members of the party awaiting arrival of the illegal liquor at the wharf; however, the officers stated they had done so as a "ruse" to keep the smuggling [shore] party from departing the area before the arrival of the State Police. *Peters* and *Jones* had each received $200 and *Wills* received $100, with a promise that another $100 would be forthcoming.

Although the officers claimed that the shore party dispersed after hearing the gunfire from the Coast Guard, today it is alleged that *Snow* had told them about the captain knowing about the delivery and, after directing *Snow* to call the State Police, they saw an opportunity to make a few bucks. Thus they told the smugglers about the State Police being dispatched.

The morning after the incident, Officers *Peters, Jones,* and *Wills* turned over the money, all $100 bills, to Captain *Webb* at the police station in the presence of state troopers and a prosecuting attorney. The bill being turned in by *Wills* was lost while in the police station. Rumor has it that Wills folded up the bill and placed it underneath the plate of his upper false teeth.

Officers *Peters*, *Jones*, and *Wills* were exonerated of any wrongdoing in the matter, and three weeks later, *Peters* was promoted to captain and *Wills* was promoted to a newly established sergeant's position.

Thus ends the saga of Groton's "Rum Running" scandal, which, even to this day, is brought to light by many "old-timers" when the subject "Prohibition" era is being discussed. ***(December 6, 2007)***

# A Distressing Fire in Groton

A little over one month ago, I watched in despair as a building on Thames Street that had housed my family's fishing tackle store burned to the ground. As I had mentioned in a previous article, the store has been a mainstay business in Groton for over fifty years and for the past twenty-two years has leased space in the building that burned.

Not only did the fire destroy a landmark business, but it also ravaged one of the oldest historic buildings remaining on that street. To say the least, the fire was a "double whammy" to me—one part being the loss of the business, which has been an intricate part of most of my life, and the second, as a local historian, the loss of a piece of Groton's historically rich buildings.

The most important thing I must mention in this article is the fact that although the building and business, as well as four upstairs apartments, were destroyed by the fire, thankfully, no one was killed or injured.

The building, located on the corner of Thames Street and the old Ferry Street, across from School Street, was built in 1897 and 1898 for Carlos W. Allyn, who was born and raised in Groton. Unfortunately no records could be found to determine who had actually constructed the building.

In the late 1880s and early 1890s, Mr. Allyn worked as a clerk at a small grocery store owned by Walter J. Starr located on Thames Street opposite Broad Street. In 1883, at the age of twenty-three, he purchased the store from Starr and continued to operate it until his new three-story brick building near the ferry landing was completed in 1898. As a note of interest, some readers may recall "The Little Big Store" on Thames Street, across from Broad Street. It was this store that was previously owned by Starr and then by Allyn. The store was torn down in the 1980s, and the site is now occupied by an apartment building.

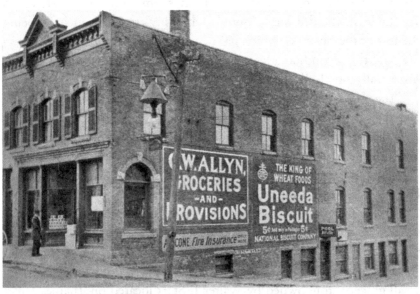

The "C. W. Allyn Grocery and Provisions" store in 1909
(Courtesy Jim Streeter)

"C.W. Allyn Groceries and Provisions" was one of the largest grocery stores in the county and, as a matter of convenience, made home deliveries throughout Groton. Because of its location next to the ferry landing, many people traveling from New London would also shop there. The grocery store was on the main level of the building, and over the years several businesses, including a paint supply store and a pool hall, occupied the basement. There is some documentation indicating that prior to the Borough of Groton building its own office building on Thames Street, office spaces were rented by the Borough on the third floor of the Allyn building. Ironically, Mr. Allyn and Alvah Cone maintained an office in the building, where they sold fire insurance.

Mr. Allyn continued to operate the store until 1924, when he sold the business to the Economy Grocery Company, Inc. This company owned several grocery stores in the county, including two others in Groton, one on Poquonnock Road near Chicago Avenue and the other on Thames Street near Eastern Point Road.

In 1931, the store was sold to the First National Store chain, and ten years later it was purchased by Nathan, Louis, and Seymour Beit who renamed it Beit Brothers.

Beit Brothers remained in business for the next ten years, until they could no longer compete with the larger box-type grocery stores, which included First National and the A & P Stores that opened in the newly established shopping districts in Groton and Mystic.

From the mid-1960s to the mid-1970s, the main spaces of the building were occupied by the Furniture Discount Village. The upstairs was converted into apartments and the bottom floor was used for storage.

From the mid-1970s through 1985, except for the upstairs apartment, the building was used for appliance repairs and as storage.

In 1985, the store became the new home of Ken's Tackle Shop, which had previously been located in the old "Groton Grain" building some five hundred feet south of the Allyn Building.

Ken's Tackle Shop—2007
(Courtesy Jim Streeter)

Although the physical properties of the Allyn Building were destroyed by the fire, the history of its occupants will live on forever. The present owner of the property has indicated his intention of rebuilding the structure. Hopefully he will keep his word, and, if he does rebuild, he will try to replicate the historical appearance of the building to make it look as it did over the previous 110 years. *(February 28, 2008)*

# Groton Monument—Lightning Strikes

A few months ago, while walking past the Groton Monument, I could not help but remember the summer night back in the late 1960s when I, as a young rookie policeman working the midnight shift during a thunderstorm, had the unfortunate experience of being in my patrol car next to the monument when it was struck by lightning. I watched in amazement as what appeared to be a ball of fire traveled quickly from the top of the monument to the ground. The flash almost blinded me. Simultaneously, the crash of thunder, which sounded to me like ten mortar shells exploding all at once, rocked me and the cruiser. I thought for sure I had just witnessed the destruction of the monument, but, to my surprise, it was still standing tall and, as far as I could determine, had not suffered any damage. Yes, the experience did scare the dickens out of me.

I went back to the police station and explained my experience to several of the "old-timers." They laughed and explained that it was not unusual for lightning to strike the monument, but it had never caused any damage.

Well, just last week, while reviewing a May 1, 1902, edition of a local newspaper, I observed the headline "Lightning Hits Groton Monument." Upon reading further, I learned that a bolt of lightning had knocked off the capstone of the apex of the monument. The granite capstone was approximately two feet square at the base, and the sides of the prism were about two feet long. It was estimated to weigh a half a ton. The lightning tore the block from its fastenings and smashed it into three pieces. It left the top of the monument flat. Man, I wished those "old-timers" were still around so they could hear about this.

The Groton Monument is without the pyramid or oblique top.
(Courtesy Jim Streeter)

This was not the first time that the top of the monument was flat. When the monument was first dedicated in September 1830, it was 127 feet tall and had a walkway on the inside of a square top. In commemoration of the centennial of the Battle at Fort Griswold, the height of the monument was increased to 135 feet and a pyramid, or oblique, top was added.

It is not known for sure when the lightning protection or grounding system was installed in the monument, but I have been told by Jonathan Lincoln, the Fort Griswold Park manager, that it is periodically struck by lightning; however, he does not know of any damage caused by these strikes since the one in 1902. *(January 13, 2006)*

# Chapter 5

## Public Safety

# Poquonnock Bridge Fire Department

During the early 1900s, several homes in the village of Poquonnock in Groton were destroyed by fire. Unfortunately, no fire system or equipment was in place, and neighbors and volunteers using the ineffective "bucket brigade" system fought the fires.

Beginning in 1914, and continuing for the next twenty years, much discussion took place concerning development of a fire system in Poquonnock. At last, in June of 1934, residents of the village signed a petition recommending establishment of a volunteer fire company and also obtaining a piece of firefighting equipment to assist in fighting fires. Shortly thereafter, on August 8, 1934, the Poquonnock Bridge Volunteer Fire Department #1 was officially organized.

Three months later, a secondhand Reo fire truck was purchased. This truck had two 35-gallon chemical tanks, 150 feet of hose, two fire extinguishers, a 20-foot ladder, and, of course, a siren. At first the truck was stored at a garage on Route 1 near the corner of Depot Road. Due to the lack of heat in this garage, the truck was subsequently stored in a heated two-story garage farther west on Route 1, close to the Poquonnock River. In addition to the truck, arrangements were made with the Groton Public Utilities to locate fire hydrants at various locations within the village.

Just after the beginning of World War II, a total of eleven hundred prefabricated homes were constructed in the village to house families of those employed to assist in the military effort. The population of Poquonnock grew dramatically, and a new and enlarged Poquonnock Bridge Fire District was created.

In January 1946, construction of the first firehouse was completed. The thirty-five-foot-by-fifty-foot wooden building was constructed mostly by volunteer labor at a cost of approximately $5,000. Later that year, the department hired its first paid driver.

The first Poquonnock Bridge fire station in June 1949
(Courtesy Janet Lester Crossman)

Over the years, with a tremendous increase in population and commercial development, as well as added responsibilities beyond just fighting fires, the Poquonnock Bridge Fire Department has expanded and developed into one of the largest and best equipped departments in southeastern Connecticut. A second and more modern firehouse was built in 1990. It is located on Long Hill Road approximately one mile from the old firehouse.

Both fire stations are fully operational and are staffed by full-time career firefighters. Volunteer firemen still play an important and strategic role in fighting fires in Poquonnock Bridge and other Groton fire districts. *(December 30, 2005)*

# Groton's Pioneer Hose Fire Company

Most in the community take for granted the services provided by the various volunteer fire departments located throughout Groton. It's hard to imagine a little over a hundred years ago, fires in Groton were fought by home owners, friends, and neighbors using the "bucket brigade" system. Too often their efforts were unsuccessful, and homes and businesses burnt to the ground. Some individuals lost their lives and others were severely injured as a result of these inadequate firefighting services.

In the late 1800s and early 1900s, the Groton Bank village of Groton was densely populated with homes and businesses. In 1900, a group of men from the village, recognizing the need for fire protection and having a deep interest in saving lives and property, founded what was known as the Pioneer Hook and Ladder [Fire] Company.

By 1901, this volunteer fire company had acquired a hand-drawn "hook and ladder truck." A wagon of sorts, this "truck" was equipped with ladders, buckets, and other firefighting equipment. It took at least twelve men to move this "truck" on level roads, and when it was necessary to move it up a hill, the first horse team that happened along would be recruited to pull it. This piece of firefighting equipment was stored in an open basement area beneath the Town of Groton's first district meeting hall, located on School Street. This building is still in existence and has been converted into a small apartment house.

In early November 1903, the Fire Company purchased a used fire hose cart for $50 from the Ockford Hose Company in New London. At the same time, the fire district committee received permission to "rent a suitable building space" to use for the storage of the apparatus and also as a place for the fire company's meetings.

Subsequently the company rented part of a barn and a store on School Street to store its equipment. It also rented a store in back of the George Hempstead's Plumbing Shop on Thames Street to use for their meetings and social events. Incidentally, George R. Hempstead was the fire chief at the time. In 1939, that building was torn down and replaced with one presently occupied by the Borough Post Office.

In 1906, the Borough's first municipal and utility building was erected on Thames Street at the foot of Baker Avenue, and the fire department was provided space in the building. For unstated reasons, the move to this building caused a dramatic decrease in the interest in the department.

In 1916, the company reorganized as the Pioneer Hose Company. They vacated the facilities at the Borough building, and they again met in a stable on School Street. By then the department had three fire hose carts. One was kept at School Street, one at an undetermined location on Monument Street, and one in a garage at the Griswold Hotel.

In 1917, the Borough built a new two-story brick firehouse on Pleasant Street. Shortly after moving into these new facilities, the department purchased its first motor-driven pumper. Membership in the fire company increased dramatically.

Over the years, more efficient firefighting apparatus were purchased and stored in the Pleasant Street Fire House.

In 1965, the City of Groton Fire Department had outgrown its facilities on Pleasant Street, and a modern and larger building was erected on Broad Street. New and larger pieces of firefighting equipment, including various boom trucks, have been purchased to fight fires at multistory structures.

Over the years, the number of volunteer members of Pioneer Hose Company No. 1 has dwindled. Today there are considerably fewer members than in the past, but those that are members are well qualified and professional at what they do. The Pioneer Hose Company No. 1 volunteer firefighters have played an important role in the history of Groton, and their services are appreciated. *(October 4, 2007)*

Pioneer Hose Company No. 1 on Pleasant Street
(Courtesy Jim Streeter)

# Eastern Point Volunteer Fire Department

During the 1940s and early 1950s, the City of Groton's Eastern Point Volunteer Fire Department maintained facilities in a building in the former Bill Avenue housing project. The project was purchased by Pfizer, Inc., in the late 1960s and is now the site of Pfizer's Global Research and Development laboratory facilities.

This photograph, taken in the early 1940s, shows several volunteer firemen proudly displaying some of their firefighting equipment. *(January 28, 2005)*

The first East Point Volunteer Fire Department facilities
(Courtesy Jim Streeter)

# Coast Guard Fire Department

Groton has always had the reputation of having a great number of fire departments protecting its residents and their property. Not only are there seven separate fire districts within the Town of Groton, each having their own separate fire departments, there are also fire departments at the Electric Boat Corporation, Pfizer, Inc., and the Submarine Base. The "mutual aid" agreement between the various fire departments within Groton has always been a plus for the community when it comes to fighting fires or assisting with other emergencies.

Most people are not aware that forty years ago there was another fire department within Groton's boundaries, the United States Coast Guard Training Station Fire Department.

Between 1938 and 1967, the United States Coast Guard maintained a training station at Avery Point on property that is now the home of a branch of the University of Connecticut.

The large number of buildings at the training station, including several wood barracks, in conjunction with the large number of men stationed at the facility, warranted the need for a fire department.

The fire department had one fire truck, which was housed in the stone building now occupied by the UCONN maintenance department. This building, prior to being occupied by the Coast Guard's fire department, was used as one of Morton B. Plant's horse stables. The fire truck, according to residents who remember it, was kept in immaculate condition.

Jack A. Eckert, who was assigned to the Avery Point Fire Department from 1958 through 1961, relayed that one of the big events every year at the training station was the annual Coast Guard Day Picnic. All the children attending the picnic were given a ride around the "big circle" in the fire truck.

In 1967, the Coast Guard moved its training facilities to Governor's Island, New York, and the fire truck was also relocated. Rumor has it that the truck was never used at the island, and it was kept outside, where it rusted away. *(November 16, 2006)*

# Groton Ambulance Association

Since officially organizing in December of 1954, the Groton Ambulance Association, Inc., has had its home at various locations throughout Groton. Their first facility was located in a modified military Quonset hut at the Trumbull Airport (now called the Groton–New London Airport) and was used to store Groton's first ambulance. Interestingly, Groton's first ambulance was a used 1946 Cadillac hearse that had been converted and modified for use as an ambulance.

In 1957, after obtaining a second ambulance, the association constructed and moved into a three-bay garage on Tower Avenue near the intersection of Thomas Road. In November 1974, the association purchased a box-style ambulance, similar to the style of the ambulances used today. Because the new-style vehicle could not be stored in the Tower Avenue facility, the Association expanded to a second facility, the old Pioneer Hose Fire Company building on Pleasant Street in the City of Groton. In 1980, the Association moved into its present and more modern facilities on Route 117, which had been constructed for their use by the Town of Groton. *(May 20, 2005)*

# The Harkness Ambulance

## Groton's First Ambulance

In the early 1940s, the Connecticut State Police Station in Groton, which was located on Bridge Street near the entrance to the Gold Star Memorial Bridge, had at its disposal a gift of an ambulance donated by Mrs. Edward S. Harkness. The "Harkness Ambulance" proved its value hundreds of times in emergencies, particularly covering points east of the Connecticut River to the Rhode Island border. *(January 21, 2005)*

The "Harkness Ambulance"
(Courtesy Jim Streeter)

# Groton's First Ambulance: An Update

Almost two years ago, in an article about Groton's first ambulance, I relayed that the first ambulance was a 1946 Cadillac and that it had been stored in a military Quonset hut at Trumbull Airport (now the Groton–New London Airport).

Recently I received information about the ambulance that conflicts with what was previously reported. I want to set the record straight, but, more importantly, I would like to pass along new and interesting tidbits about Groton's first ambulance.

In April 1947, the newly organized Groton Ambulance Service, Inc., the predecessor of the Groton Ambulance Association, purchased a used ambulance from the Hoxie Ambulance Services of Mystic for the price of $1,000. Judging by a recently discovered photograph, it appears it was an early 1930s Cadillac.

Present at the 1947 proceedings transferring the ambulance in were Groton Ambulance Services President Vito DeNoia and Hoxie Services President Louis Ravanelle. Both of these names are well-established Groton families.

After making the purchase, and in an effort to recoup the money paid for the vehicle, the ambulance was placed on display at various locations throughout Groton. It was also driven through the streets of the Borough to entice individuals to make donations or to purchase subscriptions for using the ambulance services. Subscription fees were set at $2 per family per year, and any nonsubscriber using the ambulance would be charged $8 per trip.

The newly purchased ambulance was originally stored in the garage of Jerry Cataldi on Oak Street during the summer months and at the J & R (Santacroce) Service Station on Thames Street during the winter months. The ambulance could only be used on a call from a doctor or a nurse. All of the drivers either had advanced first-aid training or had previous ambulance driving experience. In addition to the driver, one attendant and one member of the family, as well as a nurse or doctor, were to accompany the patient on emergency trips.

Groton's first ambulance
(Courtesy Hoxie Fire Department)

By the way, the ambulance on its first emergency day run was involved in a slight accident at the intersection of Poquonnock Road and Mitchell Street, after its siren failed to work. Fortunately no one in the vehicle was injured, and, after changing a flat tire, the ambulance completed its trip to the hospital.

No information is presently available to indicate the destiny of the ambulance. *(April 19, 2007)*

# Civil Defense Drill

The recent "Terrorist Drill" held at Fort Trumbull in New London is certainly not the first emergency drill to be held in the area.

In 1956, Groton also participated in a nationwide drill called "Operation Alert." Local Civil Defense and various emergency services groups from Groton participated in a simulated evacuation of Groton. The evacuation points were Preston, North Stonington, and Stonington.

Shown in this photograph, taken at a runway at the former Trumbull Airport (now the Groton–New London Airport), are the various pieces of apparatus and personnel who participated in the drill. Groups and organizations taking part in the drill included the Groton Auxiliary Police, cars and crews of the Groton Ambulance rescue and medical units, Red Cross and welfare workers, civil defense wardens, apparatus from the Groton Borough, Center Groton and Poquonnock Bridge fire departments and aircraft from the Auxiliary Police Air and Maritime Civil Air Patrol. *(April 22, 2005)*

# State Police Barracks—Groton

Groton has never seen a shortage of police protection. There are presently three separate and distinct police departments in Groton: Groton Town, Groton City, and Groton Long Point. If that is not confusing enough, it was not too many years ago that the State Police also had facilities and men assigned to Groton.

Beginning in 1921, the State Police established substations or barracks throughout the state of Connecticut. In 1923, a barracks—"Station Number 6"—was established in Groton in what was once a privately owned house on Eastern Point Road. At this time, each substation was generally manned by only one or two officers. Shortly after the "Barracks" became operational, a class of thirty-seven police recruits reported to the Groton station for their three-week police training program. This class of recruits would help the department reach its authorized strength of one hundred officers.

In 1931, the Connecticut General Assembly appropriated $15,000 for the purchase of land "at the intersections of the Norwich, New London, and Groton state highways" (now known as Bridge and Thames streets) and a sum of $35,000 to construct a new two-story brick barracks. Once the construction was completed and the barracks moved, the Eastern Point Road property once again was used as a private residence. It was subsequently purchased by Pfizer, Inc., and was razed to make room for their research and development facilities.

The first State Police barracks, located on Eastern Point Road.
(Courtesy Jim Streeter)

In 1939, the "Barracks" designations were changed from Stations to Troops. Groton Station Number 6 became Troop E.

By the late 1960s, due to increased manning and upgrading of equipment throughout the State Police, the facilities at the Groton barracks were no longer adequate. In 1973, Groton's Troop E moved to new facilities on I-395 in Montville. The old barracks at Thames and Bridge streets is now occupied by the New England Adolescent Treatment Center. *(June 17, 2005)*

The State Police barracks at the intersection of
Thames and Bridge streets
(Courtesy Jim Streeter)

# State Police Training Classes—Avery Point

A little over a year ago, I wrote an article about the State Police presence here in Groton. I explained that in 1923 a police barracks or substation was established in a privately owned house on Eastern Point Road. Then in 1931 it moved into a newly built barracks on Thames Street where the New England Adolescent Treatment Center is presently located. In the late 1960s, due to increased manning and upgrading of equipment within the State Police, the Groton barracks facility was no longer adequate. Thus in 1973 they moved to new facilities on I-395 in Montville.

The article mentioned that shortly after the State Police moved into their first barracks on Eastern Point Road, a class of thirty-seven police recruits reported to the station for their three-week training period.

Unbeknownst to many people is the fact that several other basic training classes for State Police recruits subsequently have been held in Groton. Beginning in 1966, due to a large number of police officers, both state and local, attending the police training academy located in Bethany Connecticut, it was necessary for state officials to find a second location to provide troopers their three-month basic police training course. Arrangements were subsequently made to use the training facilities at the U.S. Coast Guard Training Station at Avery Point in Groton.

At least five classes were held at Avery Point between 1966 and 1968. Members of the first three police classes shared the facilities with Coast Guardsmen stationed at Avery Point. The recruits used the old wooden barracks and classroom buildings at the base and were also permitted to use the gymnasium and swimming pool for physical training purposes. Members of the first three classes had the privilege of eating their meals at the Coast Guard Mess Hall, thus enjoying the same food served to the Guardsmen.

Although the Coast Guard moved its training facilities to Governor's Island, New York, in September 1967, the State Police continued to hold their recruit class at Avery Point. They then shared the facilities with students from the University of Connecticut.

In a recent discussion with a retired State Police officer who graduated from the Avery Point site in February of 1968, it was learned that after the departure of the Coast Guard from the facility, the recruits' meals were catered into the facility and were often cold or dried out before they arrived. It was also learned that all of the recruits had received their firearms training in a remote area at the Groton–New London Airport, where a large sand pile was located. *(August 31, 2006)*

# Chapter 6

## Landmarks

# Groton's "Submarine Capital of the World" Sign

Last October, to the chagrin of the local community, one of Groton's most symbolic and visible landmarks, the "Submarine Capital of the World" sign, was vandalized. Someone had used yellow paint to deface the sign, a large metal silhouette of the nuclear submarine *Nautilus*, with antiwar slogans and obscenities.

Almost immediately members of the Groton community, including military, government, civic, and citizenry, quickly banded together to repair this dastardly act. Within a few short weeks, all remnants of the vandalism had been removed.

History about the sign can be traced back to July of 1959 when the Groton Chamber of Commerce requested permission from the Connecticut State Highway Department to erect a sign on the south side of I-95 just east of the Gold Star Memorial Bridge. The purpose of the sign was to acquaint travelers and visitors to the fact that Groton, with its deep-rooted involvement in submarines, was the "Submarine Capital of the World." The sign, in the shape of a Lafayette class nuclear submarine, would be forty feet long and twelve feet high, and would display the words "Groton" and "Submarine Capital of the World" in colorful neon lights.

On July 19, 1963, over four years after the request had been made, the state issued the Chamber a permit to erect the sign. The reason for the four-year delay is unknown.

Once the permit was issued, the Chamber, led by its president Clarence Sharpe, initiated a campaign to raise the $3,000 needed to build and erect the sign. By April of 1964, only about a third of the required money had been raised, and consideration was given to scrapping the project. Additional funding appeals, in conjunction with a commitment from Sharpe to provide labor and equipment from his dredge and dock company to help build and erect the sign, kept the project alive. Work on the site began in June of 1964.

Visual Arts of New London, whose owner, Oscar Russell, was a longtime resident of Groton, was awarded the contract to build the sign. Using steel angle iron framing and galvanized sheet metal, Russell and his workers completed most of the project in about three weeks.

There was one delay, however. A controversy arose over the spelling of the word "Capital." Some believe the word should have been spelled "Capitol," with an "o"; others felt the last vowel should be an "a." Town Librarian Martha Hagerty had the last say and decided that it would be grammatically correct to spell the word with an "a." Once the issue was resolved, the sign was painted and neon lights were installed.

The first "Submarine Capital of the World" sign was erected in early November of 1964.

The Lafayette sign was also prey to acts of vandalism. According to Mark Russell, who worked for his father (Oscar) in the 1970s, it seemed like about every six months he was assigned to repair the neon lights after they had been smashed by rocks.

Over the next forty years, exposure to the elements caused severe deterioration to the Lafayette sign, and all agreed it was beyond repair.

In 2004, in conjunction with the upcoming celebration of the fiftieth anniversary of the commissioning of the USS *Nautilus*, the Lafayette sign was replaced with a one-eighth scale silhouette of the *Nautilus*.

Groton is proud of not only being the home of the Submarine Base, the Electric Boat Corporation, the Submarine Force Library and Museum, and the National Submarine Memorial, but also the thousands of men and women who have been part of the submarine history of our community. Groton surely qualifies as being the "Submarine Capital of the World," and our submarine sign is one way of displaying such pride. Mark Russell contributed to this article. *(August 9, 2007)*

The Lafayette class "Submarine Capital of the World" sign
(Courtesy Roadell Hickman)

# The Latham Memorial Fountain

Groton has many very visible and notable landmarks and monuments. Some more readily recognizable include the Groton Monument, the Avery Memorial, the USS *Nautilus*, the Avery Point Lighthouse, and the "Submarine Capital of the World" sign. One small but important monument, which for many years has existed in obscurity, is the Latham Memorial Fountain.

In the summer of 1902, local chapters of the Children of the American Revolution developed plans to build a memorial park on a piece of land at the intersection of Poquonnock and Eastern Point roads. The park was to honor Groton's own Captain William Latham, a defender and hero of the Revolutionary War battle at Fort Griswold. The park was to be located directly across from the Eastern Shipbuilding Company, now the home of the Electric Boat Corporation.

The plans included constructing a small building to house a reading and writing room for the workmen at the shipyard and converting a water spring on the property into a memorial drinking fountain for workers to enjoy.

Nellie Plant, wife of Groton millionaire Morton F. Plant, attended a concert held as a fund-raiser for the park. Shortly thereafter Mr. Plant offered to pay for the cost of the memorial fountain, provided it was made available for use by both man and beast. It should be pointed out that Mr. Plant himself was a Son of the American Revolution. Mr. Plant's suggestion was adopted without reservation.

John Salter & Sons Monument Company of Groton built the fountain from a large piece of granite. Its dimensions are seven feet from the bottom to the crest of its ornamental top piece and four feet in diameter. The body of the fountain is cylindrical and has a hollowed-out drinking trough of about fifteen inches. Two large shallow troughs are attached to the base for smaller animals. The smaller ornamental top piece has a dolphin carved on its face and water flowed from its mouth. Several cannonballs from the Fort Griswold battle adorn the top.

The fountain was unveiled on November 1, 1902. It was moved from the intersection of Poquonnock and Eastern Point roads to the lawn in front of the City of Groton Municipal Building in September

1968. The monument has been saved for everyone to savor. *(November 30, 2007)*

The Latham Memorial Fountain
(Courtesy Jim Streeter)

# The Rise and Fall of the John Mason Statue

Over the years, there has been a considerable amount of controversy concerning what has been called the Pequot "War" that took place on "Pequot Hill" in the village of Mystic River and the Town of Groton in 1637. During this battle, Captain John Mason led an expedition of approximately ninety men and defeated the Pequot Indians at their fort in Mystic. An estimated four hundred to seven hundred Pequots, including men, women, and children, were killed during the battle. Mason was subsequently promoted to the rank of major.

Some two hundred and fifty plus years after the battle, the State of Connecticut commemorated it by erecting a statue of John Mason on Pequot Avenue in Mystic, reportedly close to the area where the battle took place

The purpose of this article is not to discuss the merits or particulars of that war but rather to relay the details and history of the statue itself, which, from 1889 to 1995, was a familiar Groton landmark.

It is unknown why it took so many years before the idea of erecting a memorial to commemorate the Pequot War was initiated, but it is believed the idea was promoted by Rev. Frederick Denison of Mystic. The reverend suggested a "boulder monument" be used to mark the site of the battle. The New London Historical Society subsequently appointed a committee to locate the exact site of the fort and to develop suggestions as to the type of monument to mark the spot.

There was a considerable amount of divergence of opinion as to the type and style of monument to be erected. Interestingly, one of the suggestions was to have a "combined representation of the Indian and white races."

In 1887, the matter was brought before the Connecticut Legislature, and, although there was a considerable amount of opposition, a resolution was passed authorizing the governor to appoint three commissioners to procure and place a "boulder monument" on the site of the battle. Once the boulder was in place, it was directed that "a suitable bronze statue, of heroic size, of Captain John Mason" be erected on this boulder. The resolution authorized State funding for the statue not to exceed $4,000.

After the resolution was passed, the New London County Historical Society appointed a committee to solicit subscriptions for the purpose of purchasing the stone pedestal. A total of $935 was raised.

The committee subsequently purchased a twenty-three-ton block of rough-cut granite from the Smith Granite Company of Westerly, Rhode Island. A total of five models and one photographic reproduction of a model of Major John Mason were submitted to the committee to select from. Sculptor J. G. C. Hamilton of Westerly was selected to design the nine-foot-tall statue that was placed on top of an eleven-foot stone pedestal. The statue of Mason was cast at the Ames Manufacturing Company in Chicopee, Massachusetts.

The unveiling ceremony for the statue was held on June 26, 1889. A large crowd gathered as Charles E. Dyer of Norwich, chairman of the monument commission, presented the statue to then Governor Morgan G. Bulkeley. The statute was then unveiled.

For the next one hundred years or so, the statute was little more than a landmark familiar to residents and a frequent target of vandalism. Then in 1992 the Groton Town Council received a petition from a member of the Eastern Pequot Indian Tribe requesting that the statue of Mason be removed, as they felt it glorified the death of hundreds of Indians.

The Town formed a committee to evaluate the request, and after lengthy study and debate, it was recommended that the statue be relocated. The Windsor (Connecticut) Historical Society requested that the monument be moved to the Palisado Green near Mason's former residence.

In May of 1995, the State removed the statue from its Mystic site and placed it in storage. It was subsequently moved to Windsor and rededicated on June 26, 1996. A new plaque was installed on the statue that removed any reference to the 1637 Pequot War. *(September 20, 2007)*

The Mason statute in Mystic, circa 1900
(Courtesy Carol Kimball)

# Groton's Revolutionary Prisoner of War Monument

Groton has always shown its gratitude toward the members of the community who have served our country in times of war and conflict. Many markers have been erected throughout Groton to recognize those who have served our country. Some of these include the Civil War Statue and Veterans War Memorial at Fort Griswold, the World War II memorial in Mystic, the Submarine Veterans memorial wall on Thames Street, and the Veterans memorial park near the Groton Town Library. The most visible and recognizable war memorial landmark in southeastern Connecticut is, of course, the Groton Monument located at Fort Griswold. This 135-foot-tall granite monument was erected to memorialize the eighty-eight men and boys who fell during the Battle of Groton Heights on September 6, 1781.

Unbeknownst to many, there is another memorial marker relating to the American Revolutionary War Battle that took place at Fort Griswold. This particular memorial commemorates the thirty-eight men that were captured and kept as prisoners of war after the battle.

According to several accounts of the battle, after the storming of the Fort, British troops took hostage those defenders who were not injured or whose injuries did not inhibit them from walking. They were subsequently marched from the Fort to the bank of the Thames River, at the base of what is now Fort Street, to await enemy boats to come ashore to take custody of them.

They were then ordered on board three small boats and taken to a larger armed sloop. Once aboard the sloop, they were placed in the hold of the vessel, where there was a cooking fire burning. The enemy had blocked up the hatchway to the holding area, making it hot and smoky and almost impossible to breathe. After much begging, the enemy opened the hatchway and permitted one or two prisoners at a time to go on deck during the night. They were provided little to drink for about twenty-four hours, and the only food they received was comprised of hog's brain.

After three days aboard the sloop, all of the hostages were brought topside, had their hands tied behind their backs, and were practically pushed over the side of the boat to fall into small boats used to transport them to a brig or prison ship.

After a four-day voyage to New York, they were off-loaded and taken to what was called the "Old Sugar House," where they remained as prisoners for eight weeks. Subsequently there was a prisoner exchange between the Americans and British, including the hostages from Fort Griswold. The former prisoners were then taken to New Jersey by boat and released about two hundred and fifty miles from their homes in Groton. It took almost two and one half months for these heroes to travel home.

Over 175 years after the ordeal, members of Groton's Anna Warner Bailey Chapter of the Daughters of the American Revolution erected a monument to recognize the brave and heroic men.

The marker consists of a large round millstone positioned at an angle on the top of a rounded fieldstone foundation. It is located in a small park on the bank of the Thames River, across from Fort Street. The millstone is inscribed with the words "In honor of the 38 patriots who were carried as prisoners in boats to New York from this shore after the Battle of Groton Heights September 6, 1781."

Unfortunately, because of its obscure location, this memorial receives little attention. Hopefully this article has shed some light upon the heroic role these men played in the history of Groton and America. We should all be grateful. *(October 25, 2007)*

IN HONOR OF
THE 38 PATRIOTS
WHO WERE CARRIED
AS PRISONERS IN BOATS
TO NEW YORK FROM THIS SHORE
AFTER THE BATTLE OF GROTON HEIGHTS
SEPTEMBER 6.1781

Groton Revolutionary Prisoner of War Monument
(Courtesy Jim Streeter)

# The Avery Memorial Arch

A few months ago, while taking a walk along Mitchell Street in Groton, I took notice of a Groton historic memorial landmark that, for years, I had either paid little attention to or that I had become oblivious to. The structure I speak of is the large stone gateway arch at the west entrance to the Colonel Ledyard Cemetery.

Upon close examination of the arch, you will observe that the pillars had been engraved with words "Erected by Elizabeth Miner Avery"—"In Memory of Her Parents Erasamus D. Avery [and] Sarah H. Avery." The Roman numerals "MDCCCCXXIX" are also engraved in one of the pillars, which, when converted to Arabic numbers, reflect that the structure was erected in the year 1929.

Elizabeth Miner Avery, who died November 10, 1928, at the age of seventy-seven, was a lifelong resident of Groton and lived on Eastern Point Road. In her will, she bequeathed a sum of $20,000 to build a memorial arch at the cemetery as a tribute to her parents, Erasamus D. Avery and Sarah Hinckley Avery.

The Averys were one of the pioneering families of Groton, and the name pervades Groton's history. Erasamus Avery's grandfather, Captain Ebenezer Avery, was killed during the Battle of Fort Griswold, and his great-grandfather, Sergeant Rufus Avery, was taken as a prisoner during that battle.

Sarah Hinkley Avery came from Plainfield, Connecticut, and her parents were prominent in working to abolish slavery.

The stones for the cemetery gateway are a coarse crystalline granite quarried in the area of Somes Sound, Maine, and were chosen for the warm texture, rosy tint, and durability. The arch was designed by the famous New York architecture company Adams & Prentice and was erected by Groton's own stonemason company, John Salter & Son, which had offices on Thames Street near the old ferry landing.

The arch is over twenty-six feet high and twenty-seven feet wide. The opening between the two vertical columns measures thirteen feet. The design of the arch is said to be Greek in restraint.

Granite walls measuring forty-five inches tall and sixty feet in length were also erected on either side of the arch to beautify the grounds.

A formal presentation ceremony for the arch took place at the conclusion of the Memorial Day parade on May 30, 1930. A crowd of approximately two hundred attended the event. Julia Avery Bill, the sister of the late Elizabeth Avery, presented the arch to Carlos Allyn, the president of the Colonel Ledyard Cemetery Association. Mrs. Bill was the widow of Frederick Bill, another wealthy Groton resident who, in 1888, donated money to build the Bill Memorial Library in memory of his sisters. Mr. Bill later provided the money to build a new Groton Heights School, and it was his financial aid that was instrumental in enabling the construction of the Groton Congregational Church on Monument Street.

As a note of interest, in 1933, after her death, Julia Bill bequeathed an amount of $40,000 to have a small stone chapel built at the Colonial Cemetery in memory of her sisters Elizabeth Miner Avery and Cora Vincent Avery.

Although in need of a good steam-cleaning, the Avery Memorial Arch and its adjoining walls still project strength and beauty. Groton should be thankful for the generous and thoughtful gift presented by Elizabeth Avery in memory of her parents. This arch marks the entrance to the burial ground of many who contributed so much to Groton's history. *(April 3, 2008)*

The Avery Memorial Arch
(Courtesy Jim Streeter)

# Groton's Avery Memorial Park

Last week's article told the story about the fiery destruction of one of Groton's oldest and most familiar landmarks—the old "Hive of the Averys" homestead, which occurred in July of 1894. (See chapter 1.) For a period of twenty years prior to the fire, all of the town business was transacted at this house, and it is where the town's records were stored.

The house was built in about 1657 on property located just south of the junctions of Poquonnock Road and Long Hill Road. Fortunately, many of the town records, dating back to 1703, were recovered from two fireproof safes in the house.

Shortly after the fire, members of various Avery families established the Avery Memorial Association for the purpose of erecting and preserving a suitable memorial on the site of the old historical homestead. The Association was officially incorporated by the State of Connecticut in September of 1895. James Avery, Jr., the last resident of the house, who was also the town clerk at the time, deeded the land on which the house sat to the Association.

The Association wasted no time in developing the memorial, and the property soon became a small park. Stone curbs were used to outline where the house once stood, and portions of the chimneys were also left intact. Old hearthstones marked the areas where doorways were once located. In the center of the property, a twenty-three-foot-high polished granite shaft was erected as a monument to the Averys. At the base of the obelisk was a bronze tablet with a bas-relief of the old homestead. The tablet was a gift from John D. Rockefeller, founder of the famous Standard Oil Company, who was an Avery descendant on his mother's side. The granite for the shaft was quarried in Westerly, Rhode Island, and the total cost for the monument was $800. The monument was placed in position in the fall of 1895, and a public ceremony was held on the second anniversary of the fire, in July 1896.

In the late 1890s, the association decided to enhance the park by adding a likeness of Captain James Avery, the first Avery to settle in Groton, in 1656, to the apex of the shaft. Sculptor Bela Pratt, a native of Norwich, who was also an Avery descendant, designed a bronze bust of Captain James Avery.

On July 20, 1900, six years to the day after the fire, a crowd of more than five hundred, including Avery descendants from throughout the country, attended this annual [Avery] association meeting and unveiling ceremony of the bust. Trains from both directions stopped at the park to discharge passengers attending the event. Dr. Elroy M. Avery, the president of the Association, presided over the meeting, and Helen Morgan Avery unveiled the bust, which had been covered with an American flag.

As a note of interest, for many decades it was believed, even by the many Avery families, that it was Captain James Avery who had built the "Hive of the Averys" homestead in 1856 and was its first occupant. Then, in the mid-1950s, in a historical paper written by Noank resident Claude M. Chester, it was revealed that Avery was deeded land at Poquonnock Bridge on December 15, 1657, and that he neither built nor lived in the homestead house. Chester's paper was based on research conducted by Mrs. Eva L. Butler, a formidable and recognized historian from Ledyard.

Although it was documented that Captain Avery did not build or live in the homestead, it is still fitting that he be recognized as being the "founder of the Groton Averys."

The purpose of the Avery Memorial Park can best be summed up by the words of Frank M. Avery made during the monument's unveiling ceremony: "We are here to dedicate a memorial—not to any one man—but to mark a spot where the roots of a family tree took hold in New England."

The small Avery Memorial Park serves as a constant reminder of the historical contributions that the Averys have made to our community for over 350 years. *(June 19, 2008)*

# The USS Flasher *Memorial*

The World War II National Submarine Memorial at the intersection of Bridge and Thames streets is one of the most highly recognized and frequently visited landmarks in Groton.

Many visitors to the memorial are enamored with the most emotional portions of the memorial, the twenty-one granite markers displaying the names of the fifty-two submarines lost during World War II and the ten polished black granite Walls of Honor, inscribed with the names of the 3,617 submariners lost during that war. Although these displays undoubtedly warrant being the center of attention at the memorial, visitors should not ignore the mainstay of the display, the conning tower of the World War II submarine USS *Flasher* (*SS-249*).

The *Flasher* was built at Groton's Electric Boat Company and commissioned in September 1943. She sailed on her first war patrol in early January 1944 and completed her sixth and final war patrol in April of 1945. She was credited with having sunk 100,321 tons of Japanese ships during the war, the only submarine to exceed the 100,000-ton mark. She received the Presidential Unit Citation for her third, fourth, and fifth war patrols. All of her patrols were designated "successful" and she received six battle stars.

The *Flasher* was decommissioned in March of 1946 and was moored with the Reserve Fleet at Groton. She was stricken from the rolls in 1959 and sold for scrap in 1963.

In 1957, the U.S. Submarine Veterans of World War II–East pursued establishing a memorial in Groton to recognize the sacrifices of their shipmates lost during the war. In June of 1963, the *Flasher*'s conning tower, fairwater, and periscopes were given to the Submarine Veterans Association for their project.

In July 1964, the Submarine Memorial became a reality, and the conning tower, fairwater, and periscopes were placed on display at the entrance to the Navy's Nautilus Park housing area in Groton.

After years of vandalism and neglect of maintenance, the memorial was relocated to the tract of land where it is presently situated. A rededication ceremony was held on September 28, 1974. The Wall of Honor was subsequently added and dedicated in September of 1994.

Groton

The National World War II Memorial–East, including the Wall of Honor and the USS *Flasher*, is a wonderful tribute to all submariners, past, present, and future, of the United States Navy. *(June 7, 2007)*

# Chapter 7

---

# Churches, Libraries, and Schools

# Union Baptist Church–Mystic

One of Groton's prettiest and prominent landmarks is the Union Baptist Church, located on Route 1 and High Street in Mystic. The church was established in 1861 when Groton's Second and Third Baptist churches united. Shortly after the merging of the congregations, their church buildings were also united. The Third Church, which was already situated on the present Baptist Hill site, was moved back a short distance, and the Second Church building was moved from its location a little over one block away.

The original steeple of the church was destroyed during the Great Hurricane of 1938 and was not replaced until 1969. *(April 15, 2005)*

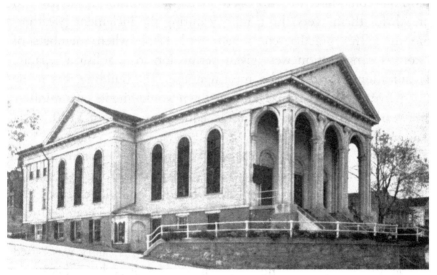

Mystic Baptist Church without steeple
(Courtesy Jim Streeter)

143

# Groton Congregational Church

On October 16th, the Groton Congregational Church will be celebrating the 105th anniversary of its beautiful fieldstone church on the corner of Monument and Meridian streets. Although many believe this was the first home for this church's congregation, it is actually the fourth.

Prior to Groton's separation and independence from New London in 1703, many inhabitants belonged to the Congregational Church on the west bank of the Thames River (New London). Transportation considerations caused great inconvenience to those who wished to worship or attend religious meetings.

In 1687, it was voted that the people on the east side of the river (Groton) could have the "liberty to invite the minister of the town to preach for them every third Sunday during the inclement [weather] months." This practice continued until 1702, when members of Groton's congregation were given permission to establish a separate organization and to build a meetinghouse. The building was to be thirty-five feet square in size, and the town would hire its own minister at a yearly salary of seventy pounds, equivalent to about $140, to be paid by the town.

The first church was erected in 1703 in Center Groton near the crossroads. Money to build the church was raised through the sale of 308 acres of town-owned land. Rev. Ephraim Woodbridge became the first minister of the church. He was well respected by his congregation, which reportedly "compose practically the entire town of Groton." He was so well liked that after ten years of service, his salary was raised to one hundred pounds and the town would "cut and cart his yearly firewood." When Rev. Woodbridge left the church in 1724 due to illness, the church had eighty-four members.

Rev. John Owen replaced Rev. Woodbridge, and within a short period of time, the congregation grew to over two hundred members.

The second meetinghouse was built in the late 1760s near Pleasant Valley. Although this building was officially named the "Kinne" meetinghouse after its minister, Aaron Kinne, it was also known as the "old black meeting house." This name was acquired when, after years of being exposed to the elements, in conjunction with the lack of being painted, the outside of the building turned black.

In 1833, the "black meeting house" was in such poor condition that it was decided to build a newer and much-larger church on Thames Street just south of the railroad bridge crossing the Thames River. The congregation remained at this location until the present fieldstone church was built on Monument Street in 1902. Interestingly, the fieldstones used to build the church were taken from several of the old Groton homesteads, including the property of Carey Latham, the first white settler in Groton; the farm of John Davie, Groton's first town clerk; and from every deacon connected with the church, including James Avery, James Morgan, and Andrew Lester, all names deeply imbedded in Groton history.

Well-known Groton residents and philanthropists Frederick Bill and Morton F. Plant, who were not members of the church, made generous donations to help pay for its construction and to keep it debt-free.

As a point of interest, the old church on Thames Street was subsequently occupied by various businesses, including a car dealership, several gas filling stations, and a Frisbie Pies distribution center. It is presently home to the Kirk Floor Covering business.

The church continues to be a mainstay of worship in Groton, and its beautiful and historic architectural features provide strong character to our community. Today the Groton Congregational Church has a congregation exceeding 250 members. *(October 11, 2007)*

Old Congregational Church on Thames Street
(Courtesy Jim Streeter)

# The Forgotten Avery Memorial Chapel

A few months ago, I wrote an article about the Avery Memorial Arch, the large stone gateway arch at the entrance to the Colonel Ledyard Cemetery off of Mitchell Street. A sum of $20,000 had been bequeathed by the late Elizabeth Miner Avery, who died in 1928, to build a memorial arch in memory of her parents, Erasamus D. Avery and Sarah H. Avery. On May 30, 1930, at a formal dedication ceremony for the arch, Julia O. (Avery) Bill, the sister of the late Elizabeth Avery, presented the arch to the Colonel Ledyard Cemetery Association.

Julia Avery Bill was the wealthy widow of Frederic Bill, who, in 1890, provided the funding to build the Bill Memorial Library in honor of his two sisters. In 1912, Mr. Bill also donated the money to build a new Groton Heights School.

Upon the death of Julia Bill in December of 1932, she bequeathed to the Hartford-Connecticut Trust Company, as trustee of her estate, the sum of $40,000 to be used for the erection of a chapel and receiving vault in the Colonel Ledyard Cemetery. The design and construction of the building was left to the discretion of the Trust Company with the approval of the Colonel Ledyard Cemetery Association. According to the will, "the structure shall be one building, built of stone … to be called 'Avery Memorial Chapel.'" It was also stipulated that a suitable table be erected upon said chapel, stating that it was erected by her in memory of her two sisters, Elizabeth Miner Avery and Cora Vincent Avery.

In December of 1933, the Trust Company and Cemetery Association approved preliminary architectural plans for the chapel prepared by the Chandler & Palmer Architects of Norwich. Ultimately, Chandler & Palmer was engaged as the architect, and H. R. Douglas & Son of New London was contracted to construct the building. Work on the chapel, which began in early May of 1934, was supervised by Thomas J. Rogers, the trust officer of the Hartford Connecticut Trust Company, and Mr. Phebe E. Gardner, chairman of the Cemetery Association's building and improvement committee.

On May 31, 1934, during a special ceremony at the cemetery, the cornerstone of the Avery Memorial Chapel was laid. The event, which coincided with the annual Memorial Day parade, was attended by more than eight hundred persons. Mrs. Gardner laid the cornerstone for the building; however, before doing so she presented a "time capsule" box to be encapsulated in the granite blocks surrounding the cornerstone. The box contained historical articles relating to the chapel, such as the names of officers of the cemetery, the name of the building, and the name of the architect.

The sixty-foot-by-thirty-foot Gothic-style building is made from granite quarried in Waterford. The roof, as well as the floor inside the chapel, is slate. The window casings and arch over the pulpit are Indiana sandstone. Four large lead-framed stained-glass windows are installed on each side of the chapel as well as one above the main entrance. The inside is adorned with a wooden cathedral ceiling and eight hand-carved pews. The total capacity of the chapel is 110—80 seated and 30 standing. There is also a stainless steel crypt in the basement capable of storing eight caskets containing bodies awaiting burial.

Construction of the chapel was completed in the summer of 1934 at a total cost of about $31,500.

A review of cemetery records indicated that the chapel, for the first five years or so, was used periodically for services for a fee of $15.

As far as can be determined through review of cemetery records and interviews of individuals associated with the cemetery and the cemetery association, the chapel has not been used for a period of over forty years. In the mid-1960s, vandals caused considerable damage to the stained-glass windows, and it became necessary to board up the windows.

On August 1st of this year, this author, with the permission of the Colonel Ledyard Cemetery Association, inspected and took photographs inside the chapel. Upon entering the building, I was amazed to find that, although it had not been used for over forty-plus years, it was in great condition. Although some moisture damage was observed around the windows, the remaining wooden ceilings, pews, and walls were in very good condition. I must mention that the electricity to the building had been shut off, and when I traveled to the basement with the aid of a flashlight, I was a little apprehensive and cautious when I opened the doors to the stainless steel crypt. Fortunately, it was not Halloween, and the batteries in my flashlight did not burn out. Oh, by the way, did I mention I was by myself?

The Avery Memorial Chapel is in great condition, considering it has not been open and/or really maintained during the past forty-plus years. Some repairs to the building and trimming of trees and shrubs close by should be taken care of in the near future to prevent serious damage. I have contacted the Avery Memorial Association and advised them of the existence of the chapel to hopefully generate some interest in restoring and maintaining the structure. Hopefully, in the near future, I can produce a slide presentation on the chapel to bring the public's attention to it. *(October 2, 2008)*

The Avery Memorial Chapel
(Courtesy Jim Streeter)

# Sacred Heart Catholic Church

The Sacred Heart Catholic Church has a long history in Groton. Church records reveal that Catholics who lived in Groton were incorporated as early as 1905. Prior to 1905, the few Catholics who were residents of Groton attended the St. Mary Star of the Sea Church in New London. From 1905 through 1912, church services were held at various temporary locations, including the waiting room at the old Ferry House on Thames Street; the Odd Fellows building on School Street, which now houses the Submarine Veterans Club; and the Town Hall on Fort Hill Road.

In 1911, Morton F. Plant, one of Groton's most affluent and prominent citizens, donated property on Eastern Point Road, across from the present-day Electric Boat Corporation. He also provided sufficient money to build a [Catholic] church and rectory. Although not a Catholic himself, Mr. Plant had brought many stonemasons from Italy, who were Catholics, to build his Branford House Mansion at Avery Point. He felt that these individuals should have an appropriate place of worship.

The cornerstone of Groton's first Catholic Church was laid on July 14, 1912. The dedication and first service in the church was held on January 19, 1913. A photograph of this church is shown below.

Beginning in the mid-1950s and continuing until the early 1960s, the church built new facilities, including the Sacred Heart School, a convent and rectory, on property located on the east side of Mitchell Street near the Colonel Ledyard Cemetery.

In May of 1961, the church and rectory property site on Eastern Point Road was sold to a contractor, who tore down both buildings and constructed what is still today a multistory parking garage. *(September 21, 2005)*

The Sacred Heart Church on Eastern Point Road
(Courtesy Jim Streeter)

# Saint Mark's Episcopal Church

The religious beliefs of the residents of Groton are, to say the least, extremely diverse. A quick review on the Internet revealed over twenty-five different churches, temples, and places of worship present within the Town of Groton boundaries.

Recently, while rummaging through my collection of photographs, I came across a picture of the Saint Mark's Episcopal Church, a quaint-looking church on Pearl Street in Mystic. Although this church is not as visible or as well-known as some others in Groton, it certainly is rich in history.

The church was developed from a mission that held services in Washington Hall beginning in 1859. For a period of four years, services were held on an irregular basis, and then in the spring of 1864 arrangements were made to hold regular Sunday night services.

In February 1865, a permanent mission was established, and the church was organized under the name of "St. Mark's Protestant Episcopal Church." There were fifteen communicants at the time of organization.

On September 12, 1865, the parish authorized the purchase of property from Captain Ambrose Burrows on Pearl Street for the sum of $500 to build a church. A building committee was appointed, and within two weeks plans were presented and approved to build a church thirty-five feet wide and seventy-eight feet long. Although work on the church commenced immediately, the unanticipated presence of ledge resulted in delays and extra costs in building the foundation.

After seven months of work, with the foundation still not complete, the original plans were scrapped. New plans were prepared, and in December 1866 the cornerstone was laid; the church opened for public worship on Christmas Day of 1867. Total cost to build the church was $9,000.

The Saint Mark's Episcopal Church
(Courtesy Jim Streeter)

One of the most memorable events of the church was the purchase of a large organ from the First Congregational Church of New London in 1870 for the cost of $500, certainly a handsome sum of money in those years.

In 1873, a $400 addition was added to the church to accommodate the large number of individuals attending the Sunday school program. On January 18, 1883, the church purchased a house across the street to serve as a rectory.

The church remains in pristine condition and maintains its original New England architectural appearance. It is one of Groton's picture postcard buildings. *(May 17, 2007)*

# *The Groton Public Library*

Groton certainly is fortunate to have one of the finest public libraries in Connecticut. Until 1960, citizens of the town relied on library services provided by the Bill Memorial Library, located on Monument Street in what is now the City of Groton, and the Mystic & Noank Library, located on Liberty Street on the Groton side of Mystic, both of which were privately owned.

Along with the large increase in Groton's population that took place in the early 1950s came an equal demand for library services. To meet the ever-increasing demand for library services, Town officials decided to establish a public library in the former William Trail School, located on the north side of Fort Hill Road near the Poquonnock Bridge Firehouse, was converted to the first Groton Public Library. The same building is presently occupied by Groton's Human Services Department.

The library consisted of several rooms, including a children's reading and book room; the main room, which housed the bookshelves, discharge desk, and card catalogue; a reference room; and study rooms. At the beginning the library was only open on a limited basis—1:00 to 9:00 PM Monday through Thursday and 9:00 AM through 5:00 PM on Fridays and Saturdays. A total of approximately six thousand books, including fiction and nonfiction adult books, children's reading materials, and standard reference works, were shelved and available at the library at its beginning.

The grand opening ceremony for the library was held on July 5, 1960. Officials of the newly established Groton Lodge of Elks conducted their first public event by presenting the library with a recently authorized fifty-star American flag to commemorate Hawaii becoming the fiftieth state of the Union.

The first Town of Groton Library
(Courtesy Jim Streeter)

Over the next fifteen years or so, the library outgrew itself. The increase in circulation and the growing size of the number of books being maintained at the old converted school warranted a larger and more modern facility. Thus, in September 1977, Groton opened its new library, located on Route 117, on property that was previously the home of the Bridge Drive-In Movie.

In the mid-1980s, a new addition was added to the library, making it one of the largest and most advanced libraries in the state of Connecticut. When one compares the present library building with the first one, it can only be said, "We've come a long way." *(January 11, 2007)*

# The Bill Memorial Library

Since publishing the "Didja Know" article about the Groton Public Library, several readers have asked about the history of another popular Groton library, the Bill Memorial Library.

Frederic Bill, a Groton native who was born in the area of the town now known as Ledyard, became very wealthy while working in his family's publishing business in Springfield, Massachusetts, and later as the owner of a linens import and manufacturing business in New York City. In 1880, Bill retired at the age of forty. He returned to Groton and purchased a large farm on Eastern Point Road where the Amerada Hess Corporation is presently located.

In October 1888, Bill announced his desire to establish a library in memory of his two sisters, Eliza and Harriet. Shortly thereafter Bill purchased over seventeen hundred books for what was to become Groton's first library. Space for the library was provided in an upper room of the First District schoolhouse, the first [wooden] Groton Heights School. The library opened on November 20, 1888.

Within eighteen months of the opening of the "school" library, Bill provided funding to have a new building constructed near the Groton Heights School and next to the Groton Monument. This elegant building was dedicated on June 18, 1890, and was appropriately named the Bill Memorial Library in honor of Bill's two sisters.

In 1907, two additions were added. One provided space to accommodate several thousand additional volumes of books, and the second provided space for a "natural history" museum. Interestingly, items displayed in the museum included Bill's extensive collection of rare butterflies and two large cases containing various mounted birds belonging to his brother Gudon. The butterfly collection is still at the library, and the bird displays are now at the Denison Pequotsepos Nature Center in Mystic.

In 1994, another large addition was added to the library to provide space for a children's room, offices, and a public restroom.

Today the Bill Memorial Library maintains over twenty thousand items in its inventory, and, although smaller in physical size, it provides almost all of the services available at Groton's main public library.

Funding for the library is provided through an endowment fund established by Mr. Bill and various donations.

Groton owes a debt of gratitude to Mr. Bill for his generous donation of this wonderful library as a memorial to his loving sisters. *(March 29, 2007)*

# The Mystic-Noank Library

The Mystic-Noank Library on the corner of Liberty and Elm streets in Mystic is one of the most attractive landmarks in the area. It was the second public library to be built in Groton and was a gift from Captain Elihu Spicer.

Captain Spicer, who was born in Noank in 1825, a shipmaster and ship owner, first went to sea at the early age of nine. By the time he was twenty-two, he became master of the bark Fanny. He subsequently mastered various clipper ships and other vessels engaged in trade around the world.

In 1861, he became a copartner of a shipping and steamship business with Charles Henry Mallory, also a native of Mystic. It was this business that brought him his fortune.

The captain had a winter home in Brooklyn, New York, and a lavish summer home on Elm Street in Mystic. In 1891, he announced plans to donate money to have a library built on Elm Street across from his residence.

Construction began in 1892 and was completed in 1894. The total cost of the building was approximately $90,000. Unfortunately, Captain Spicer died while the library was being built, and he did not get to see the fruits of his gift. In his will, he provided for the completion of the building and also for the acquisition of four thousand books.

Only the best of materials, including Roman brick, Connecticut granite, and marbles from Vermont and Africa were used to build the library.

The building opened to the public on January 30, 1894. The first floor was used as a meeting/lecture room and the second floor as the library.

The popularity of the library grew in leaps and bounds. By 1924, the number of books had more than doubled. In 1951, the library was moved to the first floor, and in 1961, it became necessary to move the children's section to the second floor.

In December 1991, a new six-thousand-square-foot addition was dedicated at the library. This additional space provided the physical facilities necessary to meet the challenges of the twenty-first century and to store additional items.

Financial support for the library is provided through an endowment fund and various donations.

A sincere debt of gratitude is due to Captain Spicer for providing Groton with this beautiful and resourceful facility. *(May 3, 2007)*

# Eastern Point School

Beginning in the mid- to late 1890s and continuing for a period of approximately twenty-five years, children living in the Groton Bank and Eastern Point areas of Groton attended a small two-room wooden schoolhouse located off of Eastern Point Road. The school was situated on what was called the Captain John Spicer property, near the intersection of Bayview Avenue in the area where, years later, the Victory Package Store was located. In the early 1920s, after the closure of the Groton Iron Works Shipyard, the school ceased operations. The building was subsequently purchased and converted into a private residence. Pfizer, Inc., now owns the property.

The present Eastern Point School on Shennecossett Road was built in 1919. Additions were added to the building in 1925 and 1941–43 and 1955. It is anticipated that use of this school will be discontinued in late 2007 or early 2008 upon completion of the new elementary school off of Poquonnock Road near Trail's Corner. *(February 10, 2006)*

The wooden Eastern Point schoolhouse in the early 1900s
(Courtesy Jim Streeter)

# The First Robert E. Fitch High School

As renovations are about to begin at the Robert E. Fitch Senior High School, it is only fitting to take a look at just how Groton acquired its high school.

As long ago as 1922, the Town of Groton felt the need to build a high school, and a committee was established to investigate its feasibility. Unfortunately, in early 1923, the suggestion to build the school was rejected.

Prior to Groton having its own high school, pupils desiring higher education would travel to schools in the neighboring towns of New London, Norwich, and Stonington. It is interesting to note that a high school existed in Mystic; however, for reasons unstated, Groton residents refused to send their children "to the other side of town."

In May of 1926, Groton merchant Charles P. Fitch died, and, in his will, he bequeathed the "residue and remainder of his estate," estimated to be approximately $50,000, to Groton to build a high school for Groton. He stipulated the school be built in Poquonnock Bridge, near the site of the Town Hall and, more importantly, it be named after his son, Robert E. Fitch, who had died in 1922. Robert Fitch, a bachelor who had served as the Borough of Groton Tax Collector, died at age fifty-three. Very little is known about the person for whom the school is named.

Construction of the two-story brick school began in August of 1928 and took approximately one year to complete. The total cost to build the school was approximately $260,000. By the time the school was completed, it was discovered that the amount of the Charles Fitch bequeath had grown to almost $100,000.

A grand dedication ceremony for the school was held on September 5, 1929.

In the mid-1950s, Groton adopted the junior high system. A new senior high school was subsequently built at the top of Fort Hill and named the Robert E. Fitch *Senior* High School. The original school was renamed the Robert E. Fitch *Junior* High School. *(September 23, 2005)*

# The Second Fitch High School

During a recent tour of the new addition at the Fitch Senior High School, I could not help but reminisce about the school as it was in the early 1960s. Many on the tour were amazed to learn about the school initially being a "campus-style" facility and its construction being an instrumental part of Groton's adopting a middle/high school system.

In the early 1950s, in an effort to cope with dramatic increases in student enrollment in the Groton schools, Town officials and the Board of Education elected to establish a junior high and high school system. This new program combined seventh- and eighth-grade classes from the elementary schools and the freshman class from the high school into the junior high. This system required building new high and junior high schools and also converting the Fitch High School into a junior high.

In September 1955, after more than one year of construction, the new Fitch Senior High School opened its doors to 550 students and a faculty of 33 teachers. The school was built on a seventy-seven-acre site on the top of Fort Hill at a cost of $1,083,000.

The twenty-four-classroom campus-style school consisted of five separate single-floor buildings. The main building housed the gymnasium, auditorium, cafeteria and kitchen, administrative offices, a classroom, an art room, and a music room. The remaining four units contained classrooms and laboratories.

Photograph of Fitch Senior High School in the 1950s
(Courtesy Jim Streeter)

The auditorium had a seating capacity of five hundred, and about eight hundred spectators could be accommodated on folding-type bleachers in the gymnasium. Unfortunately, shortfalls in funding precluded the auditorium and gymnasium from being outfitted with the seats and bleachers during the initial construction phase.

Although the "campus-style" facility was considered "state of the art," in practical terms it had its drawbacks. Because each building contained classrooms for different subjects, students had to walk some distances on blacktop and plywood walkways between buildings in all types of weather. For some of us, the travel allotment provided us time to smoke a quick cigarette. Yes, with verified permission from parents, smoking was permitted in designated areas.

Three units were added to the school in 1958 and 1963. Construction projects during the 1970s and '80s connected all of the buildings and increased the number of classrooms to sixty-two.

Although the new construction phase at the school includes razing the old units, good memories of their existence will live on for many years to come. *(June 28, 2007)*

# The Fitch High School Seal

Recently, my friend Carol Kimball, who is Groton's town historian, asked for some help in answering an inquiry she had received from a teacher at the Robert E. Fitch Senior High School who was trying to determine the background of the symbols in the school's official seal. More specifically, the teacher asked what the "creature" was at the bottom of the seal.

It was coincidental that recently, while looking through my collection of Groton ephemera, I had come across a document depicting the school's seal and also providing some details about the seal's symbols. With tongue-in-cheek, I must admit my own embarrassment that, as a graduate of Fitch and having looked at the seal many, many times, I, too, knew very little about it.

To begin, I think it would be best to explain how the school got its name.

In May of 1926, Groton merchant Charles P. Fitch died, and, in his will, he bequeathed the "residue and remainder of his estate," estimated at the time to be approximately $50,000, to Groton to build a much-needed high school. He stipulated that the school be built in Poquonnock Bridge, near the site of the Town Hall, and, more importantly, it be named after his son, Robert E. Fitch, who had died in 1922.

Construction on the two-story brick school was completed in September of 1929 at a cost of about $260,000. Not too bad if you take into consideration that a new high school built in the mid-1950s cost about $1.1 million, and recent modifications and an addition to that school cost $45 million. The first high school was subsequently converted into the Fitch Middle School.

It is not known exactly when the school's seal was designed and adopted, but, according to a graduation program for the school's "Class of 1933," it was explained that the seal "embodies the history of the town of Groton as well as the Fitch family coat-of-arms."

The lighthouse and beacon at the top of the seal represents the seafaring days of the town and also symbolizes the influence of the school on the lives of future citizens. The outline of a shield is an adaptation of the Fitch family shield. In the upper left-hand corner of the shield is a drawing of the tip of the Groton monument that was erected to commemorate the men who died in the Battle of Fort Griswold. In the upper right portion of the shield is depicted the hilt (handle) of the sword of Captain John Mason, who led the 1637 Pequot massacre in Mystic.

Below these two figures is a wide chevron, which is part of the Fitch family coat of arms that represents "protection, builders or others who have accomplished some work or faithful service." Quite a fitting symbol, if you ask me.

After doing a considerable amount of research on the Internet, it was learned that the "creature" symbol below the chevron is a lion's head, and it too is part of the Fitch family coat of arms. All of the Fitch family coat of arms that were pictured on the Internet contained three lion heads, two above the chevron and one below. The lion head represents bravery, strength, and valor.

After providing the above information to the teacher who made the inquiry, he indicated that he was now going to pursue producing a large graphic of the shield, which will also contain an explanation of the seal's symbols.

Incidentally, below the seal in the 1933 graduation program were written the words "Education is a lighthouse by the eternal tide of life." How true! *(June 26, 2008)*

### The Fitch High School Seal

Shortly after writing the article describing the Fitch High School seal, I received a telephone call from Robert Welt of Mystic, who relayed that it was his father, Simon A. Welt, Jr., who had designed the original school seal. Simon subsequently worked at the Electric Boat Company as a designer and also took over the reins of his father's store, "Welt's Meat Market," on Thames Street. *(August 21, 2008)*

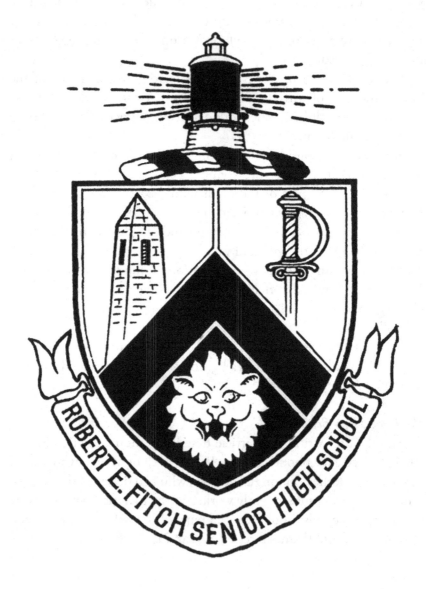

The Robert E. Fitch High School seal
(Courtesy Jim Streeter)

# Chapter 8

## Businesses

# The Sister Banks of Mystic

Prior to 1800 and until about 1810, the commercial hub of Mystic was located at the head of the Mystic River in the vicinity of what is now called Old Mystic. It was during this period of time that Old Mystic was known as "Mystic River." In 1830, the name was changed to "Mystic," and in 1890, it took on the name "Old Mystic."

In 1833, the first Mystic bank was chartered by the State and established in Old Mystic. Soon after it was chartered, the bank built a small granite stone banking house in the center of Old Mystic. In 1856, the bank acquired land nearby where they constructed and occupied a larger brick facility. Both of these buildings still exist today. The first building was moved to the Mystic Seaport Museum, where it remains on display, and the second is presently the home of the Indian and Colonial Research Center.

Beginning around the late 1840s, the commercial and industrial center slowly began moving away from Old Mystic to a point farther south down river called Portersville, which today is known as "downtown" Mystic. In 1851, Portersville was renamed Mystic River, and in 1890, the word "River" was dropped from the name. The increase in commerce and industry in the area created a great need for a new commercial bank.

The need was filled in 1851 when the Mystic River Bank was organized. In 1852, the bank built and opened new banking facilities on West Main Street in what is now downtown Mystic.

A few years later, in 1854, some men closely associated with the Mystic River Bank organized the Groton Savings Bank. Both banks, although operating under different charters, shared the same banking facilities.

In 1865, after the passage of the National Bank Act, the Mystic River Bank became a national bank and changed its name to the Mystic River National Bank.

By 1930, both banks had outgrown the building they were sharing, and it was agreed that they would construct a new structure large enough to allow for future growth. Temporary facilities were secured, and the old building was torn down. A new and modern building was constructed on the same site.

The new Georgian Colonial–designed structure was built of Indiana limestone with a granite base. It has a frontage of seventy-two feet on the square at the foot of what is known as "Baptist Hill." At the time, the bank boasted of having one of the finest vaults of its kind in the state. The walls of the vault had an intricate system of steel rods with concrete poured around them and an interior lining made of steel one-half inch thick. The vault was secured at night with a twelve-inch-thick steel door that was equipped with three movement time locks and safety devices. It was also protected with a system of electrical sound accumulators that would sound an alarm should any attempt be made to bore through the walls. Pretty impressive for any small-town bank, if you ask me.

In 1954, the Groton Savings Bank moved from West Main Street to new facilities on the corner of Water and Main streets. It is now the home of Chelsea Groton Bank.

The Mystic River National Bank Building, built in 1931, still stands today and is occupied by the Bank of America. *(April 17, 2008)*

The Mystic River National Bank building from 1851 to 1931
(Courtesy Jim Streeter)

# Groton's Quinnipiac Fertilizer Company

Prior to the mid-1800s, New England farmers always believed the only affordable fertilizer they needed to use to raise their crops was manure from their stables.

All of this changed when new scientific methods were developed to produce affordable fertilizers that were proven not only to produce rapid and healthy growth of crops but also increase crop yields. Many of the new fertilizers were being produced from the bony remains of menhaden fish after they had been processed for their oil for the tanning industry.

The Quinnipiac Company, which became one of the largest manufacturers of fertilizers in the United States, commenced business as a firm in Wallingford, Connecticut, in 1852. In 1871, the company incorporated with an office in New Haven. Then, in 1877, the business moved its headquarters to New London and established new and modern manufacturing facilities on Groton's Pine Island, located just off the shore of Eastern Point.

Within a short period of time, the company had erected thirteen buildings on Pine Island, and the enterprise became the largest of its kind in the state. The average annual output of fertilizers was ten thousand tons, worth more than half a million dollars. Fifty men were employed at the factory. Transportation of raw materials and manufactured goods was also a large part of the business and indirectly furnished employment to many others. As an example, more than four thousand tons of fertilizers were shipped via the railroad each year.

The company processed menhaden fish oil at the plant and used large quantities of the fish scrap that remained to produce various fertilizers. Raw materials, such as blood and bones from other fish companies in the West, potash from Germany, and sulfuric acid, were constantly delivered to the island for use in manufacturing fertilizers.

Some of the products sold under the name Quinnipiac included "Potato Manure," "Market Garden Manure," "Fish and Potash," "Lawn Dressing," and "Dry Ground Fish Guano." Yes, there was even a product called "Pine Island Phosphate," which, according to the company's brochure, was recommended for growing corn, wheat, rye, and oats. This product reportedly had an "enviable reputation" in the South of producing superior and large crops of cotton.

The company continued its operations on Pine Island until the early 1900s. As the story goes, after Morton F. Plant built his mansion at Avery Point, he soon became annoyed with the odor emanating from the small island a short distance from his back door, and, thus, in 1903, he purchased the island and all of its buildings. It has been said that Plant had the buildings removed and a five-hundred-tree orchard planted in their place.

It is interesting to note that the use of fish as a fertilizer diminished in the early 1900s as new synthetic fertilizers were introduced onto the market. Thus, the sale of the Quinnipiac Fertilizer Company to Mr. Plant was a timely move. The company went out of business shortly thereafter. *(July 12, 2007)*

# A Third-Generation Family Business

Not too many businesses in New London County can boast of having been operated by three generations of the same family. One business that can do so is Byles-MacDougall Funeral Service.

The business was started by Robert Hooker Byles, who was born and raised in Norwich. After graduating from Norwich Free Academy, he worked for seven years as assistant with different undertaking firms in Norwich. In 1903, he began an undertaker business in Lewiston, Maine.

In 1906, Byles came back to New London and established his funeral business at 52 Main Street. He remained there until January 1920, when he moved into a house he had altered and added to at 15 Masonic Street. Also the same year, he married M. Hortense Eagles, and they had three children, including Robert Everett, who, in 1934, joined the business with his father.

In 1938, the business moved to its present location at 99 Huntington Street in New London. The business was named Byles Memorial Home.

At the beginning of World War II, Robert (the son), was activated into the Army and left the business to fight in the war. Shortly after this, John T. MacDougall, the stepson of Robert H., joined the business.

It should be noted that in October of 1927, a little over a year after the death of his wife Hortense, Robert H. remarried, to Maude MacDougall, who had children from her first marriage.

After the war, Robert (the son) rejoined the business with his father and stepbrother John T. In 1948, the business was incorporated and became "Byles-MacDougall Funeral Services, Inc." The business had expanded to include many customers from Groton, where the Byles family resided.

Shortly after the death of Robert Byles (the father), in 1952, it was decided to convert the Byles family "homestead" at 310 Thames Street in Groton into a funeral home. The Groton home opened in 1954.

In 1971, Donald Byles, the son of Robert E., after graduating from Bryant College and the San Francisco College of Morticians, began a two-year apprenticeship with his father and uncle and became the third generation to join the family business. In 1979, John D. MacDougall, the son of Duncan MacDougall, joined the business, also becoming part of the third generation in the business.

Robert E. Byles died in 1974, and John T. MacDougall died in 1999.

A few things of interest that should be mentioned in this article are the facts that funeral services provided by Robert Hooker Byles in 1903 were $45 ($30 for the casket, $10 for embalming, $3 for the wagon, and $2 for a shave). Somewhat shocking when you consider that the average cost of a funeral today ranges from $5,500 to $7,500 or even higher. Oh, by the way, according to Don Byles, his grandfather got "stiffed" (no pun intended) when he didn't receive payment for the services.

The second, and more important, bit of information to include in this article is the fact that Don Byles's daughter Mackenzie is presently in her second year at the New England Institute of Arts and Sciences at Mount Ida College taking studies in Funeral Home Management. Who knows—she just may be the fourth generation to join the business.

In the bygone days, words such as "Undertaker," "Mortician" or "Embalmer" were used to define or describe the person or business responsible for making arrangements for the transportation, burial, or disposal of a person after his or her death. Well, in today's politically correct world, the person is called a "Funeral Director" and the business is referred to as a "Funeral Home." Although the business does not appeal to everyone, the majority of funeral directors today are educated professionals who take great pride in their abilities and the services they provide. The people at the Byles-MacDougall Funeral Services have, over the past one hundred years, proven their commitment and provided comforting and appropriate funeral services. Don Byles contributed to this article. *(May 8, 2008)*

# Thames Street—The Former Hub of Groton Businesses

The history of Groton can be traced back to 1646, when John Winthrop, Jr., settled on the Thames River and established a plantation on both sides of the river called New London. Within twenty-five years, various fishing and coastal vessels and boats were being built in the village located on the east bank of the river. The primary means of travel from one side of the river to the other was the ferryboat, and the first ferry landing on the east side of the river was built in the area known as "Groton Bank." The presence of the shipbuilding trades, in combination with the easy accessibility to the ferryboat landing, caused neighborhoods of people and many small businesses to spring up along the eastern shore. For the next three hundred years, the main street of Groton Bank, which ran parallel to the east side of the Thames River, was a primary business district for the residents of Groton. Originally called Bank Street, that road is today known as Thames Street.

Of course, up until the appearance of the motorcar in the early 1900s, and continuing until the time of the trolley, the primary means of transportation was by horse or oxen. It was commonplace to see men and women riding single horses or horse-drawn carriages. Wagons, both large and small, drawn by teams of horses or oxen, traveled up and down the road to make deliveries or to pick up various materials and supplies. Yes, even horse-drawn stagecoaches would be seen on an almost daily basis traveling to and from the ferry landing.

Although, by today's standards, the dirt street was narrow, the horses, oxen, carriages, wagons, and coaches usually had no problem traversing the road.

By about 1910, the business district of the Bank was blooming, and trolley cars were added into the mix of transportation on the street. For years the horse-driven and trolley car modes of transportation coexisted on the narrow street with very little problem. Then in the late 1920s and early 1930s, a third method of travel, the automobile, was added to the street, making traveling on that street a little more congested.

With the increase in the use of automobiles, the use of horses and oxen diminished considerably.

Initially, parking of vehicles was permitted on both the east and west sides of Thames Street. The narrow width of the street, especially in the prime business areas between Latham and Broad streets, caused some traffic tie-ups and frequent "sideswipe" damage to vehicles.

Shortly after the beginning of World War II, with the increase in defense-related work at the Electric Boat Company, the traffic on Thames Street became almost unbearable during the peak traffic hours when workers were traveling to and from the shipbuilding facilities on Eastern Point Road. Although public parking for merchants and shoppers was permitted in the old ferryboat landing area off of Ferry Street, across from School Street, parking on both sides of the street contributed to the congestion and accidents.

In May of 1944, the Borough of Groton's (now the City of Groton) Board of Warden and Burgesses voted to prohibit parking on the east side of the street. Many business owners were up in arms and protested the measure. John Couch, the owner of the then Groton Hardware Store and a well-respected civic volunteer, became spokesperson for the merchants. The group he represented contributed the most to the traffic "snarls" and fender scratch incidents due to an unreasonable speed. They also indicated that the public parking lot was not being used to its fullest. They suggested that the speed on the street be reduced and the public be made aware of the public lot.

Mr. Couch also made comment that the parking bans could, over a period of time, cause customers to avoid the inconvenience of the parking restrictions and to shop elsewhere.

Ultimately, a compromise was struck, and parking was again permitted on the east side of Thames Street, but only during no peak traffic hours and only for a period of five minutes.

Beginning in the mid-1950s and continuing until today, parking on the east side of Thames Street from Pleasant Street to Broad Street is prohibited.

As a point of interest, fifty years ago, seventy different businesses made their home on Thames Street. Today there are only thirty-four. Was Mr. Couch right?

The present study being conducted by the City of Groton to rebuild

Thames Street as well as to revitalize the once-flourishing business district is of interest to many residents in Groton. The fact that over four hundred residents signed a petition against making the street one-way for vehicular traffic is encouraging, as it does reflect interest. If this interest can be channeled into suggestions as to ways to revitalize the street, then the study is not for naught. This historic business district needs the public's help. *(October 23, 2008)*

The Coe & Bailey Store and WMCA facilities on Thames Street around the turn of the century. The bottom floor is today occupied by Thames Army Surplus.
(Courtesy Jim Streeter)

# Witch Hazel

I wonder how many readers will recall seeing a bottle bearing the name "Witch Hazel" in the medicine cabinets of their parents or grandparents. What was contained in the bottle was a patented herbal medicine that, at one time, was considered to be one of the best remedies for sore muscles, cuts, insect bites, irritations, inflammation, and even tumors. This so-called magic medical potion was produced from the stems and bark of the common American shrub called *Hamanekus verbakus*, ultimately nicknamed Witch Hazel, which grew in abundance in Connecticut.

Thomas N. Dickinson, a Baptist minister, was instrumental in commercializing and manufacturing the witch hazel extract in facilities in Essex, Connecticut, in the late 1870s.

During the period from 1911 through 1917, his son, Thomas N. Dickinson, Jr., who resided in Mystic, produced what was called the Ledyard Brand Witch Hazel from a distillery in Groton. The distillery was located on Poquonnock Road, just west of the former Henry Trail School on property now occupied by the Groton Utilities Water Treatment Facility.

Most of the witch hazel plants used at the distillery were harvested from property where the water treatment facility is located. It is ironic that branches from witch hazel plants were also used as divining or dowsing rods, which were commonly used to search for underground water sources. *(March 10, 2006)*

The old Witch Hazel building in Poquonnock Bridge
(Courtesy Jim Streeter)

# Ken's Tackle Shop

Not too many stores in Groton can boast of being in business for fifty-plus years. One such business, Ken's Tackle Shop, located on Thames Street near Paul's Pasta, is celebrating its fiftieth anniversary this month. I should be up-front with the readers by saying the story of this business is of interest to this writer because it is owned and operated by my family.

In the early 1950s, my father, Ken Streeter, an avid sports fisherman, began producing ("tying") and selling artificial fishing flies from our home in Poquonnock Bridge. Shortly thereafter his custom-made fishing rods and other fishing equipment were added to the items he was selling. It reached the point where one of the three bedrooms in the house was transformed into a fishing tackle store of sorts.

In March 1957, my father, who was also employed at the Electric Boat Company, decided the bedroom had outgrown its part-time business status and that it was time to open a full-time tackle store. He selected a site on Thames Street close to various fishing locations and on a road traveled by many fishermen going to their boats and launching facilities at Eastern Point.

Due to the fact that my father was employed full-time, my mother, Callie, learned the business and ran the store during the day. At the end of his workday, my father would relieve my mother and keep the store open for another three or four hours. Since most of the customers worked during the week, weekends became the busiest time for the business. On many weekends, the entire family, including myself, could be found working at the store.

By the early '60s, the business had blossomed to the point where my father gave up his full-time job. For years thereafter, my mother and father kept the business open seven days a week and, with the exception of Christmas Day and maybe a few days in the winter, it was open year-round.

Ken Streeter holding a fishing lure at his store on Thames Street.
(Courtesy Jim Streeter)

In 1972, after my father passed away, my sister Dottie started working at the store and within a few years became the manager. My mother continued working at the store until shortly before her death in 1998. Dottie continues to operate the store, and it still maintains the reputation of being one of the finest fishing tackle stores in southeastern Connecticut. *(March 22, 2007)*

# Groton Cigar Factory

For approximately ten years, the author of this article has had in his collection two prized wooden cigar boxes displaying the words "Groton Cigar Factory, Groton, Conn." printed on the paper labels inside. Attached to the outside of each box is a warning cautioning persons not to use the box for cigars again. Certainly this is a less serious notice than the health warnings appearing on tobacco containers of today.

Until very recently the only information that could be obtained as to the location of the factory was "somewhere on Thames Street." In September of this year, while talking with longtime Thames Street resident Tony Levesque, he produced a blueprint drawing of his family's property on that street. In the drawing, dated 1906, was the property identified as "The Groton Cigar Factory." Based upon the drawing, we determined that the factory had been located at what is now 181 Thames Street, the location of the Hell-Cat charter fishing boat business.

Although specific information as to the dates of operation could not be determined, Carol Kimball, Groton's town historian, relayed she had found mention of the factory in two small "Groton Doing's" sections of the June 12, 1902, and September 12, 1903, editions of the [New London] *Day* newspaper.

Little else is known about the Groton Cigar Factory. Anyone who may have additional information is encouraged to contact the author through the *Groton Times* to assist in filling in the blanks of this interesting facet of Groton's business history. *(November 25, 2005)*

A wooden Groton Cigar Factory box
(Courtesy Jim Streeter)

# Johnson's Hardware Store

Almost everyone who has grown up in Groton over the past sixty years is familiar with the name "Johnson's Hardware." Located on Fort Hill Road near the intersection of North Road in Poquonnock, the hardware "general store" has been owned and operated by the Johnson family since the mid-1920s.

Actually, in the beginning it was not a hardware store. In the early 1920s, William A. Johnson, who worked as the yardmaster for the Midway train facility in Poquonnock, and his wife, "Lu," conceived the idea of opening a small gasoline and lunch business. While on vacation in Maine, the Johnson's visited a store called "KUM-SEE-ME" and were so intrigued with the name they paid a handsome fee of $25 for permission to use the name for their business in Groton.

In 1925, Groton's KUM-SEE-ME Filling Station opened for business. While her husband worked at the train facilities at Midway and New London, Lu ran the business. Originally there was only one gas pump and the lunch business served only coffee and sandwiches; but by the time the Fitch High School was completed in the late 1920s, business was booming. The station expanded to four pumps and the lunch business mushroomed when students from Fitch began to hang out there. The store also began to sell groceries and ice cream.

In the early 1950s, William A.'s son, William D., purchased the business. He increased the grocery business, added a meat department, and opened a hardware store in the basement.

By the mid-1950s, the hardware store had become so popular, a forty-foot-by-one-hundred-foot addition was added. In 1966, a second addition, to accommodate a home and garden rental business, was added. One year later, a third addition was added. The store had grown to over forty-eight thousand square feet, and Johnson's two sons, William E. and Thomas, joined the business. Although the size of the business increased, it always maintained its friendly and neighborly atmosphere.

The "KUM-SEE-ME" store with Lu Johnson and
her two children, William D. and Gert
(Courtesy Johnson family)

In May of 1981, a tragic fire destroyed the business. Fortunately, the Johnson family did not throw in the towel. Within one year, a new building was constructed and Johnson's Hardware and Home Center was back in business. It continues to be one of Groton's last family-oriented businesses. *(February 15, 2006)*

# The Atlantic Coast Fisheries Company

In 1927, the Atlantic Coast Fisheries Corporation of New York established a fish processing plant in Groton on the site of the old Groton Iron Works, now the home of Pfizer, Inc. It ultimately became the largest fish filleting and processing plant in the world.

Up until the mid-1920s, if one wanted to enjoy the distinctive and delicious flavor of fish, it needed to be consumed while it was fresh. Keeping the fish fresh so it could be shipped to areas away from the shores where it was caught was impractical. More distant markets depended upon curing the fish with salt or using ice to refrigerate it. These techniques subtracted from the flavor of the fish, and, if it was not preserved quickly and properly, the fish would spoil.

In the early 1920s, the Atlantic Coast Fisheries was experimenting with the technique of quick freezing fish products to enable the product to be shipped to consumers in distant markets. At the same time, the company's research group had discovered a new brine that successfully sealed in the flavor of fish that had been lost during the quick-freezing process. By employing both of these new techniques, the fish product could be preserved for indefinite periods of time, and at the same time the flavor was in as excellent a condition as when the fish was caught. Called "Nordic Fillets," the new process revolutionized the production and consumer aspects of the fishing industry.

By 1927, the production of the Nordic Fillets had increased so much that the Atlantic Fisheries purchased the Groton Iron Works shipyard in Groton. Within one hundred days, part of the plant was transformed into what was considered the "largest filleting and processing plant in the world."

Production of the Nordic Fillets increased from one hundred thousand pounds in 1927 to over twenty million pounds in 1929. Net earnings of the Atlantic Coast Fisheries Company went from $116,357 in 1925 to $1,052,430 in 1928.

A fleet of twenty-three radio-controlled fishing trawlers, seventeen out of Groton and five from Canada, supplied the plant with fish. The fish were unloaded from the boats into large metal bins and then transported via conveyors to the filleting processing facilities. The fish bones, skins, and waste materials were removed and later vacuum-cooked into valuable cattle and poultry feed. Within fifty minutes of being filleted, the fish were processed and frozen. After being frozen, the filets were either sealed in fifteen-pound packages or sent through a "staking machine" that punched out round slices of steaks of uniform size, weighing exactly one-half pound. The steaks were then packed in pairs in cardboard and cellophane packages and shipped to ninety-five cities in thirty-six states via a fleet of twenty-five specially outfitted refrigerator railroad cars.

The Fisheries employed many local residents, and it has been said that the income of the employees was frequently supplemented with fresh fish.

The Atlantic Coast Fisheries Company remained in Groton until the early 1940s, when it moved its operation to New York. The property was sold to a Norwegian industrialist who had plans of building a $20 million fleet of freighters. Unfortunately, these plans never came to fruition as the federal government took over the property to build submarines. It subsequently became known as the "Victory Yard." In 1946, the Chas. Pfizer Company purchased the property. *(July 12, 2007)*

The Atlantic Coast Fisheries Company with two fishing trawlers tied up at its docks.
(Courtesy Jim Streeter)

# The Chrissos Poultry Farm

Who would have thought that back in the 1920s through the 1950s Groton was home to one of the largest and most modern poultry farms in New England—the Chrissos Egg and Poultry Farm.

The farm was established in 1919 by Christopher Chrissos, who had previously worked as the assistant manager at Morton Plant's Branford Farms in Groton, a farm that will be the subject for a future "Didja Know" article. The Chrissos farm was located on property on the north side of Grove Avenue.

Mr. Chrissos started his farm in a small way, beginning with approximately two hundred hens and a small poultry house. The farm grew in leaps and bounds, and by the early 1930s it had become one of the largest poultry farms in Connecticut. More than five thousand [chicken] layers and breeders were kept on hand at all times. Approximately ten thousand chicks were also raised in the farm's thirty brooding coops to ensure a constant replacement of the layers and breeders. The egg-laying portion of the farm required six facilities, each of which were twenty feet by eighty feet. There was also a large two-story "egg laying" building, measuring twenty-four feet by two hundred feet that was considered one of the most modern poultry facilities in the country. This building was not only ventilated, but was electrically lighted and equipped with feed carriers, fertilizer cleaners, and automatic water fountains. It also had grain elevators and a sanitary dropping pit. In its peak time, the farm spread out over fifty acres of land between Grove Avenue and the Pleasant Valley Road.

The Chrissos farm also maintained incubator facilities for fifty-five thousand eggs and would ship out over one hundred thousand baby chicks by parcel post each season throughout New England. The farm was the primary producer of white eggs. The bulk of the eggs were used by the Mohican Hotel and sold by the Mohican market in New London. In addition to Mr. Chrissos, the farm employed five full-time employees.

The modern two-story "egg laying" building on the Chrissos farm
(Courtesy Dorothy Chrissos)

In the early 1940s, a large portion of the farm's land was acquired through "eminent domain" by the U.S. Government to build many of the Navy housing units.

In the late 1940s and early 1950s, poultry "factory farming" made an impact on the business, and Mr. Chrissos elected to cut back on the number of layers and breeders he kept. In the late 1950s, after running the farm for almost forty years, Mr. Chrissos decided to retire and to discontinue the business. *(November 2, 2006)*

# G. M. Long & Co.

Beginning in the early 1900s and continuing for a period of over fifty years, one of the most recognized names in the retail and wholesale fish business in New England was G. M. Long & Company. Originally located in New London on the Thames River near the Union Railroad Station, it was sold to the J. A. Young Company, a large commercial fishing company out of Boston. Because of name recognition, the company remained G. M. Long & Co.

Shortly after the sale, the new owner asked Arthur Greenleaf, a resident of Maine who had worked fishing and lobster boats for years for the Young Company, to "take a shot" at running the new business in New London.

Subsequently, Mr. Greenleaf moved to the area and operated the business. Around 1915, Greenleaf and "Nat" Avery purchased the business from J. A. Young. In 1920, after Mr. Greenleaf became the sole owner of the business, it was decided that the shores in Groton were better suited for operating the business and storing lobsters. Thus, the building in New London was moved to Groton off of Thames Street, across from Pleasant Street.

Due to Mr. Greenleaf's keen business sense, the operation grew in leaps and bounds. The customer base was extended to cover restaurants along the shore all the way to Branford and into Rhode Island. G. M. Long & Company also provided fresh fish products to all of the military bases in the area. During the peak business season, the business employed ten to fifteen employees. Several family members, including three of Greenleaf's sons and a brother-in-law, were employed in the business.

The 1938 hurricane destroyed the building that had been moved from New London. A branch building located on Bridge Street was moved to the Thames Street location to keep the business in operation. Shortly after the end of World War II, a wooden barracks that had been used by an anti-aircraft artillery unit at Fort Griswold was moved in pieces and rebuilt at the fish market location on Thames Street.

G. M. Long & Company in about 1948
(Courtesy Jim Streeter.)

In 1945, after returning from military service, Greenleaf's youngest son, Arthur, Jr., went into business with his father. In 1947, the elder Greenleaf died, and the business was taken over by Arthur, Jr., who kept the business running until it closed in 1957. Some of the business's buildings still remain and are being used for storage. Arthur Greenleaf, Jr., contributed to this article. *(August 10, 2006)*

# Jamestown Ferry Restaurant

Back in the early to mid-1970s, one of the most unique places to eat in Groton was the "Ferry Restaurant," which was located on the Thames River off of Fairview Avenue and almost underneath the Gold Star Memorial Bridge. The restaurant was physically located on the *Jamestown Ferry*, a boat which had previously been used to transport passengers and vehicles between Newport and Jamestown, Rhode Island.

In the late 1960s, shortly after the first highway bridge was completed that connected Newport and Jamestown, the ferry was placed up for sale at auction. Clarence B. Sharpe, the former mayor of the City of Groton and owner of the Whaling City Dredge and Dock Company in Groton, who was very shrewd and ingenious at his business, wanted to purchase the ferry for use in the disposal of wooden pilings and planks from the dock at the Navy Submarine Base. According to Sharpe's son Robert, the Sub Base was going to remove and replace wooden piers at the Submarine Base, and his father was going to place a bid to remove and dispose of the creosote-treated wood. His plan was to purchase the ferry, remove the top decks, and then fill the remaining sections with sand. He would then take the ferry out to sea and use it as a burning platform for the wood removed from the piers.

Mr. Sharpe's company did not win the contract to remove the piers; however, he subsequently came up with an alternative plan for the ferry, which incorporated four different ventures: a restaurant, a homeport for a river tour boat business, a souvenir store, and a picture gallery about submarine history.

The restaurant opened in 1970 and was operated by Jerry and Judy Williams. At first it was a cafeteria style that catered to the people who went on the river tours or who visited the picture gallery. Within a few years, the restaurant was converted into a sit-down French-cuisine-type facility which attracted tourists and local residents. A lounge with a piano bar was also added.

Clarence Sharpe died in 1974, and all of the businesses associated with the ferryboat closed in 1975. The ferry was subsequently sold and used in New York City. *(June 29, 2006)*

Jamestown Ferry Restaurant
(Courtesy Jim Streeter)

# Groton Bank & Trust Company

Prior to April of 1953, residents of Groton had to travel to either New London or Mystic to do their banking.

In the fall of 1951, the Groton Chamber of Commerce, under the direction of two of its presidents—John L. Couch, owner and operator of the Groton Hardware Store on Thames Street, and William J. Bartinik, owner of Bartinik's Grocery Store on Poquonnock Road—named a committee to conduct a preliminary study to determine if there was an interest in establishing banking facilities in Groton. Gilman C. Gunn spearheaded the committee.

The initial survey indicated that there was widespread support for the bank idea. At first the Mystic National Bank was approached to open a branch in the central Groton area; however, they declined.

Subsequent to the Mystic bank refusal, the committee pursued creating an entirely new bank with funds provided by people in the town.

In October 1952, bank organizers filed corporation papers to establish the Groton Bank & Trust Company, and in a little over one month, the bank was granted a temporary charter.

Once the charter was received, the newly appointed board of directors of the bank leased and renovated a building located at 486 Thames Street that had previously housed "Bill & Mill's Market," which was owned and operated by William and Carmella Tischer.

The building is presently the home of the Riverfront Children's Center.

On April 25, 1953, the bank officially opened. Free gifts were given to all visitors on opening day, and special gifts were provided to those who opened accounts of $5 or more. Other than the normal services offered by other banks, the Groton bank boasted of being the first bank to offer a "Sidewalk Window Service."

The bank's popularity grew in leaps and bounds. Within three years, due to inadequate space in the bank building, it was necessary to rent three other nearby buildings. When the five-year lease was up in 1957, the bank moved into larger and more modern facilities at 738 Long Hill Road in the Groton Shopping Plaza.

Groton Bank & Trust Company at 486 Thames Street
(Courtesy Jim Streeter)

The Groton Bank & Trust Company was subsequently acquired by the Connecticut Bank and Trust Company and the name "Groton" was no longer used. *(January 6, 2006)*

Much of the information in this article was provided by Virginia Robarge and Shirley (Rabitaille) Viveiros, who both worked at the Groton Bank & Trust Company when it was on Thames Street.

# Maxson Brothers—Hardware and Lumber Store

It was not too many years ago when home owners and contractors obtained their home improvement and building needs at small local hardware and lumber stores. Many such "mom and pop" businesses were located throughout Groton. Names such as Groton Hardware, Groton Lumber, Johnson's Hardware, Campbell's Hardware, Aben Hardware, and Diamond Lumber Company were all household names for local contractors and family "home repairers."

In the late 1930s, two Groton brothers, Norman and Silas "Brud" Maxson, who were building contractors, saw the need for a lumber store in the central area of Groton. Thus in 1938 they opened the Maxson Brothers Lumber store on Long Hill Road. In a short period of time, the store gained popularity, and it was expanded to carry various hardware and home improvement items.

Unfortunately, in 1942, shortly after the beginning of World War II, it became more and more difficult to obtain merchandise to sell, and it became necessary to close the store. Both brothers immediately went to work at the Electric Boat Company to help in the war effort.

After closing the store, the building was occupied by several different businesses, including the Ashawog River Mills, a fabric store. The Village Bake House and Grader's Jewelers presently occupy it. *(January 27, 2006)*

# Chapter 9

## Recreation

# Groton Long Point Casino

In the early 1920s, Groton Long Point was developed as a beach community. It was formally chartered as the Groton Long Point Yacht Club in 1934. From its beginning, the Club has strived to provide recreational and other social activities for its members and all other residents of the Point.

Although an exact date cannot be established, it is believed that in the late 1920s or early 1930s, the Club constructed a large "community center"–type facility to hold many of their different recreational and social events. The building, called the "Casino," was centrally located in the Groton Long Point district.

The building housed a small bowling alley on the first floor and a large dance and meeting hall on the second floor. Some of the activities held at the Casino included children and adult dances, bingo, movies, banquets, and various community meetings. It has also been said that during the 1930s and 1940s, church services were held in the building.

The original Casino was completely destroyed during the hurricane of 1938 but was quickly replaced with the present "Casino" building the following year. *(April 13, 2006)*

The Groton Long Point Casino prior to 1938 Hurricane
(Courtesy Jim Streeter)

# Electric Boat Diesels

On Sunday, February 5th, millions of Americans will have their eyes and ears glue to televisions to watch one of America's most viewed programs, the National Football League's fortieth Super Bowl. Surely thousands of "Grotonites," old and young, will be among the viewers.

Many Groton residents are probably not aware of the fact that in the 1940s and continuing until the mid-1950s, Electric Boat fielded a semiprofessional football team comprised of workers at the shipyard. The team, called the Electric Boat Diesels, would play other semiprofessional teams throughout New England. Partly due to their reputation as a very good football team, in November of 1943 an agreement was reached for an exhibition game between the Diesels and the Green Bay Packers of the National Professional [football] league.

Over ten thousand spectators attended the game, which took place on Sunday, November 28th, at the then Muzzy Field in Bristol, Connecticut.

During the first quarter of the game, the Diesels played exceedingly well and kept Green Bay in check. At the end of the quarter, the score was Green Bay 7, Diesels 0. Because they were having trouble scoring on the ground, Green Bay began a relentless passing attack and pretty much scored at will. The Diesels did not score until the last quarter when the score was 55-0. The final score was the Packers 64 and EB 14.

The following morning, the Packers team took a train to Philadelphia, where, the next weekend, they walloped the Philadelphia Eagles. The EB team members reported back to work at the shipyard to build submarines for the war effort. *(February 3, 2006)*

# Groton's "Driving Park"

Back in the days called the "Gay Nineties," a term referring to the decade of the 1890s, when our country experienced rapid economic expansion, entertainment facilities in Groton were sorely lacking. Movie theaters and nightclubs were nonexistent. There was, however, another form of entertainment established in Groton during that period of time that quickly became a popular place to spend Saturday afternoons. Believe it or not, it was a "race track."

The Groton Driving Park, as it was called, opened in 1892 and remained a viable entertainment enterprise for the next twenty years or so. Located in Poquonnock Bridge at the base of Fort Hill on the south side of what is now Route 1, it was on property now occupied by some of the Fort Hill Homes and Sutton Park.

The idea of building a track was conceived in 1890 by several local "sporting" men who had an interest in racing their horses. Interestingly, prior to the building of the track in Poquonnock, a favorite winter sport was horse racing on the ice on Long Pond in North Stonington. The Groton Driving Park Company was officially organized and incorporated in December 1891.

One month following its incorporation, the company leased a tract of land approximately twenty acres in size from Henry Gardiner of Waterford for $50 a year. The lease agreement required that the company keep the grounds groomed, but it also contained two unusual contingencies: (1) a prohibition against shooting or destroying game birds or animals and (2) prohibiting the sale of beverages containing more than 20 percent alcohol.

What was considered one of the most professional and groomed tracks in the country was built at the park. It was a half mile in length, level on the straightaways with slight railroad grades at the curves. Most of the track was fifty feet wide except that it was sixty feet wide from the last turn, down a 630-foot homestretch, and past the judges' stand. The entire track was enclosed with a high board fence. The grandstand held six hundred people and provided a complete view of the entire track and everything taking place on it.

Besides trotters and harness racing, the track was also used for bicycle races and later automobile racing. The park also featured facilities for picnic outings, baseball games, and other field events. Because of its location, people from throughout southeastern Connecticut found it convenient to travel to the park. Many people also took special excursion trains from New London and Westerly, Rhode Island, that traveled to Poquonnock's Midway Station, a three-minute walk from the park.

Admission to the races was fifty cents, and children accompanied by parents were admitted free. During the first few years of operation, it was not unusual for crowds ranging in numbers from twelve hundred to twenty-five hundred to attend the usual Saturday afternoon events at the park.

Beginning around 1910, interest in the track diminished greatly, and over the next five years or so, several attempts were made to rekindle interest in the park. Although there were sporadic times when attendance at the park was high, by 1915 the owners felt it was not financially feasible to keep the track in operation. Unfortunately, by 1917 the driving park ceased to exist, and Groton lost one of its most interesting recreational facilities. *(July 26, 2007)*

The Groton Driving Park
(Courtesy Mystic Seaport)

# Washington Park

Washington Park is located in the City of Groton district of the Town of Groton. It is considered by many to be one of the finest outdoor recreational areas in southeastern Connecticut.

Back in the early 1900s, the property was a combination of farm pastureland, swampland, and a public dump.

As early as 1919, the owner of the property, George Marquardt, and his sons, began converting the land into a park of sorts. They graded over a portion of the dump with dirt and made a rough but suitable area to play baseball.

In the 1930s, George Marquardt and his brothers Charles and Christian saw a need for a recreation area in Groton and donated twenty-nine acres to the Borough of Groton, which is now called the City of Groton. They stipulated it be called Washington Park, after President George Washington, and that a skating pond be maintained on the property. The skating pond was subsequently named "Lake George" in memory of George Marquardt, who died shortly after donating the land.

Various semiprofessional baseball teams have played at Washington Park. In the 1940s, baseball Hall of Famer Lawrence "Yogi" Berra, who was stationed at the Groton Submarine Base, played ball there, and it was here where he was reportedly scouted and recruited for the New York Yankees.

The park also hosted circuses and carnivals and, for many years, was used for fireworks displays. Today the park provides facilities for various sporting and recreational activities. What was once a dump is now a recreational jewel of Groton, thus lending credence to the saying "One person's junk is another person's treasure." *(October 14, 2005)*

# Groton Town Beach

Many people believe that the present Esker Point Beach was the only beach operated by the Town of Groton.

Long-term residents, including the author, recall the first Groton Town Beach, the one located on the west side of the Poquonnock River at the north end of the Groton–New London Airport. Entrance to the beach was gained via a mile-long access road off of South Road. As best as can be determined, it opened in the summer of 1953. The warmth of the water was a welcome habitat to both the swimmer and the stinging marine species called the "jellyfish." The large abundance of the fish at the beach caused the Town to erect offshore nets to keep the "stingers" from reaching the swimmers. Unfortunately, the nets did not trap all the jellyfish, and bathers were often heard complaining of being victims of the fish. Jellyfish aside, the beach was enjoyed for many years by swimmers, picnickers, and boaters.

In 1970, due to the implementation of the "instrument landing system" at the airport, access to the beach was eliminated. Thus concluded the existence of the first Town Beach.

This picture shows the beach club building at the Town Beach, which housed restrooms, a concession, and a community/entertainment room. *(September 16, 2005)*

The Groton Town Beach (Courtesy Jim Streeter)

# Eastern Point Beach

In July 1945, the Borough of Groton, now the City of Groton, appointed a committee to find a suitable location to establish a public beach in Groton. Subsequently six locations were considered: the small park area at the end of Fort Street, Chapman's Beach at the south end of Electric Boat, two parcels in the Jupiter Point section of Eastern Point, the Gardiner property at Bluff Point, the privately owned Shennecossett Beach in Eastern Point, and the privately owned property of William, Eleanor, and Susan Tyler in Eastern Point.

After conducting thorough studies of each location, the committee selected the Tyler property as best suited for purchase and development of a beach. Subsequently the four-and-one-half-acre property, comprised of a twenty-three-room premise and a barn with an apartment, having approximately two thousand feet of water frontage, was purchased for the market price of $40,000. Quite a bargain when you consider today's standards.

This photograph shows a "For Sale" sign on the Tyler property prior to its purchase by the Borough of Groton. *(July 22, 2005)*

The Tyler House at Eastern Point Beach
(Courtesy City of Groton)

# The Shennecossett Golf Course

The Shennecossett Golf Course had its beginning in 1898 when Thomas W. Avery, a farmer who lived in the Eastern Point area of Groton, constructed a four-hole golf course on his farm property.

With the assistance of Morton F. Plant, one of Groton's richest and most influential residents, the course was expanded to become a nine-hole course in 1906–07. Mr. Plant wanted this expansion to be completed to coincide with the opening of his new luxurious Griswold Hotel in June 1906. It is believed the course was again expanded in 1911 to eleven holes.

Between the period of 1911 and 1914, Plant acquired land to permit expansion of the golf links, and by 1914 Shennecossett had become an eighteen-hole course. Two years later, the course affiliated with the United States Golfers Association.

The first clubhouse at Shennecossett was a wooden structure similar in style to the present-day Spanish-style masonry building, which was constructed in 1914.

The golf course was privately owned and operated until November 1968, when the Town of Groton purchased it for a price of $900,000. In the late 1990s, after a land swap between Groton and Pfizer, Inc., the fifteenth, sixteenth, and seventeenth holes of the course were relocated to the former property of the Griswold Hotel overlooking the Thames River. The golf course is ranked within the top five in the state of Connecticut. *(June 3, 2005)*

Golfers on the eleventh green and the golf club in the early 1920s
(Courtesy Jim Streeter)

# Groton's Bluff Point Camping Colony

Of all the recreational facilities available in Groton, the Bluff Point State Park and Coastal Reserve has to be considered an "environmental treasure" for everyone to enjoy.

As you stroll through the 778 acres of pristine forest, wetlands, and beachfront on Long Island Sound, it is hard to imagine that almost seventy years ago, there was a thriving camping resort of sorts on the property.

Although the property at Bluff Point is rich in history and can be traced back to the mid-1640s, in the interest of keeping with the basic story of this article, we will jump ahead to 1881, when the property was conveyed to Henry Gardiner of Millstone Point in Waterford. Incidentally, Gardiner purchased the property, believed to be approximately twelve hundred acres, for $12,700. In 1907, the Gardiner family rented Bluff Point to Groton's John Ackley for what was said to be $1,000 per year. Ackley raised beef cattle, pigs, and sheep on the property and in later years grew potatoes. He became one of the largest potato producers in Connecticut and Rhode Island.

During the early years of Ackley's occupancy, Bluff Point became a popular area for picnics and camping. According to Groton town historian Carol Kimball, "during the early 1920s, Bluff Point became a campers' paradise."

By the late 1920s, many individuals approached Ackley seeking permission to build or move cottages or shacks onto the property overlooking Fishers Island and Long Island sound. Because the terms of his lease permitted subleasing, Ackley rented sites for the cottages for a nominal fee of $25 per year. The lessee was required to erect and maintain his own building.

By the mid-1930s, the Bluff Point cottage colony had grown to well over one hundred buildings. Although most of the buildings were considered to be shacks, there were also several large cottages. The summer colony blossomed into a "community" of sorts. There was what was known as the "Blue Shanty," a refreshment stand where you could buy candy and ice cream and rent canoes and rowboats. Then there was the "casino" or pavilion, where dances were held on Wednesday and Saturday nights. On Sundays, church services were held at what was called Sunset Rock at the point.

Beginning in the mid-1930s, rumor had it that the Gardiners were considering selling the property to the State of Connecticut to be converted into a state park or to be developed into an exclusive summer resort.

In June of 1938, the legal representatives of the Gardiner family issued notice to the owners of all of the cottages advising them to terminate using the buildings by October 1st and to remove their building from the land by November 1st. Any building remaining after that would become the property of Henry Gardiner, Jr.

Ironically, before it was necessary to remove the cottages, the Great Hurricane of 1938 struck Connecticut head-on. Bluff Point was no match to the force of the hurricane, and when it was over almost all of the cottages had been completely destroyed. Needless to say, this was the beginning of the end of the "Summer Colony at Bluff Point." *(August 16, 2007)*

Some cottages at Bluff Point
(Courtesy Anne and Alan Bentz)

# The Renowned Camp Mystic—A Summer Camp for Girls

Some ninety-plus years ago, one of the finest and most systematically organized girls' summer camps in the eastern United States flourished on the west bank of the Mystic River. Named "Camp Mystic," it was established by Mary L. Jobe, the famous and distinguished woman explorer and naturalist. The mission of the camp, according to literature provided to prospective attendees, was "to produce fine, big-minded, strong, healthy girls, to carry on and supplement all the good influences of home, school and church."

In the summer of 1914, Ms. Jobe, who was looking for the ideal place to establish her summer camp for girls, was invited to spend a weekend in Noank visiting her friend, noted artist Henry Ward Ranger. During her stay, she paid a visit to the former property and temple where the once-famous and greatly attended Universal Peace Union meetings were held on the River Road. The ten-acre tract, originally known as "Fish Grove," was about a half mile north of Mystic village, across the river from the Elm Grove Cemetery. The property, which was no longer being used by the Peace Union, was available for purchase. Feeling that the site would be an ideal, ready-made location for her girls' camp, Ms. Jobe purchased the property in October of that year.

Beginning in the summer of 1916 and continuing until 1930, Camp Mystic would become the home of eighty-plus girls for the summer months of July and August. Activities provided during their stay at the camp included training in camp crafts, swimming, diving, boating, arts and crafts, nature study, patriotic service, horseback riding, dancing, and field athletics.

Attendees were assigned to two groups, seniors and juniors. Juniors were from eight to thirteen years of age, and seniors were from fourteen to sixteen or seventeen. Consideration for group assignments was also based upon experience and adaptability. The girls were under constant and direct supervision of a stall of counselors and expert instructors personally selected by Ms. Jobe.

Girls attending the camp were provided accommodations in spacious canvas "tent bungalows," sixteen feet square, with wooden frames and floors. Each had windows on their side and a wide double door at each end. The camp also boasted of having a complete system of flush water toilets with the best of sanitary methods and also the luxury of shower and tub baths. It should be noted that in my research there was no mention of having hot water for the shower or baths.

The camp had several buildings, including a large two-story structure with a large "living room" with an open fire, a spacious roofed-in pavilion measuring 100 feet by 120 feet, an assembly hall and library and a large open fire, a glassed-in sun parlor on the sides of this building that could be opened or closed dependent upon the weather, and a large dining hall. The pavilion also served as the "life center" of the camp. It was here where all social functions, including dances, festivals, entertainment, musicals, and plays, were held.

Much of the activities at the camp were physical in nature. Besides daily swimming and diving, the girls participated in games such as basketball, tennis, baseball, volleyball, and kickball. Then there were the frequent "tramping and camping" expeditions on Fishers Island and one-day trips up Lantern Hill in Ledyard. Another exhilarating and enjoyable program at the Camp was horseback riding.

The girls were also provided training in various arts and crafts, including basketry, pottery, weaving, knitting, and embroidery. There were also classes in nature studies of plants, flowers, trees, birds, and stars. Music and dancing were also considered an important part of the summer program. Camp songs became part of the daily routine, and instruction was provided in various forms of dancing.

"All work and no play" was not the norm at the Camp. There was a variety of entertainment each evening, including plays, music, dances, and storytelling by girls attending the camp. Periodically a well-known author or musician would provide special entertainment. On occasion Ms. Jobe would also give talks about her exploration activities.

The camp was much regimented and almost militaristic in nature. A "Typical Daily Program" schedule appearing in a catalog for the camp reminded me of my military days: "Rising Bell" (6:45 AM); "Breakfast" (7:30 AM); "Tent Inspection" (9:00 AM); "Assembly – Mail" (9:15 AM); "Dinner" (12:30 PM); "Supper" (5:30 PM); "Entertainment" (7:00 PM); "Retiring Bell" (8:00 PM); "Silence Bell" (9:00 PM). Also, all those attending the camp were provided a list of required clothing items to bring with them to ensure "uniformity of costume" for camp unity and attractive appearance.

The all-inclusive fee for attending the eight-week camp back in the 1920s was $375. Although it seems like a bargain, by today's standards its cost would be equivalent to over $8,000.

After the 1930 season, largely as a result of the Great Depression, the number of applicants for the camp was so low that Mary Jobe decided to close Camp Mystic. Mary Jobe died in 1966. Her will provided that the property be placed in trust for a nature preserve.

Today, the property is a "Peace Sanctuary," under the stewardship of the Denison Pequotsepos Nature Center. The public is encouraged to visit and enjoy this wonderful nature preserve, which is opened daily during daylight hours. *(November 20, 2008)*

# Connecticut Defenders Baseball Team

The recent announcement changing the name of the minor league baseball team in Norwich from the "Norwich Navigators" to the "Connecticut Defenders" does southeastern Connecticut proud.

Not only does it bring attention to the recent efforts to remove the New London Naval Submarine Base from the federal base closure list, it also brings to light the fact that many of those who have been stationed at the submarine base have participated in the recreational game of baseball.

During World War II, many men assigned to the base had temporarily interrupted their careers as professional baseball players so they could serve their country. There were others who placed their hopes of being professional baseball players on hold until after the war. The pool of baseball talent assigned to the base was sometimes beyond belief. It was often said the teams representing the base were "semipro," and they were scouted by representatives of various professional baseball teams.

The notoriety of the baseball players assigned to the base was beyond compare. In fact, many of the players had contact within the pro ranks and would invite famous players to participate in special baseball events held at the base.

It seems appropriate that the "Connecticut Defenders" has chosen for its logo a baseball bat resembling a submarine, which represents the major role that the submarine base plays in our southeastern Connecticut. More ironic is the fact the "Connecticut Defenders" is an affiliate of the San Francisco Giants. In 1945, during the final stages of World War II, several members of the then New York Giants, the predecessor of the San Francisco Giants, visited the Groton Sub Base, including Giant outfielders Leon Treadway, Charlie Mead, Danny Gardella, Mel Ott, and John Rucker. *(November 11, 2005)*

# Chapter 10

## Miscellaneous

# Noank's "Muse" Island

Sometime ago, while my wife and I were having breakfast with our friends Bob and Lillian Iron, I mentioned that I was doing some research on Noank's Mouse Island. Bob then relayed he recalled there once being some controversy about the island being called "Muse" not "Mouse" Island. From all I had been told and from the research I had conducted up to that point, the island's name was "Mouse."

For those readers who are not familiar with the island, it is located just southeast of the Morgan Point Lighthouse on the south end of the village of Noank. It encompasses a total of a little less than 1.5 acres and is divided into three properties. You would have thought, because of its small size, that it would be listed in the Guinness Book of Records as being the "world's smallest island." Surprisingly, and maybe even incorrectly, it is not. Bishop Rock, an island of about two acres, having only one structure, a lighthouse, holds the Guinness record. Maybe someone having a little time on their hands could pursue this with the Guinness officials? But, on second thought, there is a small half-acre island at the mouth of the Thames River on which someone has built a home.

Although not officially documented, it has been said that the Mashantucket Indians originally owned the island and used it to dry their fishing nets. It was part of a reservation that the colonists subsequently acquired in a land swap involving a few thousand acres of land in Ledyard where, reportedly, the casino is. The earliest Groton land record for the island shows it being deeded to Captain John Ashcraft in 1731. Over the next one hundred and fifty years, the property changed hands several times. In 1881, it became the property of Nelson Morgan. All of the land records specifically document the island as being "Mouse Island."

As the story goes, in 1897, Herbert L. Mitchell, an Episcopal minister from Yantic, who had previously ministered at a church in Mystic, and his friend George V. Sevin purchased the island from Morgan for a sum of $50. Not too shabby when you take into consideration that today's combined land assessments for the island properties total almost $1.4 million.

The island was subdivided into three plots, and Messrs. Mitchell and Sevin built small homes on their properties located at either end of the island, with the center piece being used as a buffer. For the next thirty-plus years, as the properties changed hands, several other houses were built. By the spring of 1937, five houses were on the island. The Great Hurricane of 1938 took no mercy on the island, and all five structures were swept away.

Three owners subsequently built new houses and cottages on the island, but in 1954 another hurricane struck the coast and caused severe damage to the three houses.

Three newer houses have been built and remain on the island today.

Now, let's get back to the original issue of this story: trying to determine if the name of the island is "Mouse" or "Muse."

It seems that a friend of the Sevin family, sea captain Gustavus L. Green, who also wrote for the [New London] *Day* newspaper, did not care for the name "Mouse Island." The name did not appeal to him, and he felt it to be too ordinary. He attempted to convince Messrs. Mitchell and Sevin to change the name to Muse Island; however, they could not be persuaded. Captain Green took it upon himself, possibly feeling it to be "editorial privilege," to refer to the name "Muse" in all of the articles he wrote for the newspaper. Some real photograph postcards picturing the island were produced around the turn of the century and incorporated the name "Muse Island" into the picture. One must wonder if Captain Green may have had something to do with them.

Three homes still remain on this picturesque Noank treasure, and, thanks to the tenacity of Messrs. Mitchell and Sevin, they did not submit to Captain Green's request and kept the name "Mouse" as the name of the island. It is hoped that the name will live on forever. *(March 27, 2008)*

# The "Wood-Allyn" and "Old Gungywamp" House

Quite some time ago, while looking through an old scrapbook in my collection, I came across a *Day* newspaper article titled "One of Oldest Houses in New England Stood in Groton More Than 250 Years; Moved to Clintonville About Year Ago" (quite a lengthy headline if you ask me). The article, which provided a detailed account about the resident's house, indicated that originally it had been located on the west end of Groton's Pleasant Valley Road near part of what was known as the Gungywamp swamp. Unfortunately, the date of the article was not present; however, after reading its contents, it was estimated that the article was probably printed in the mid- to late 1930s. That, of course, meant, if the house was still standing today (2008), it would now be over 325 years old.

Ownership of the land on which the house was built was traced back to 1650, when it was "granted" to William Wellman. The property was subsequently sold to Joseph Nest, a weaver, whose wife was the sister to Walter Buddington of Groton. According to the *Day* article, Nest built the house in late 1678 or early 1679.

Various write-ups provide a description of the large wooden house. It is two stories in the front and one in the back, giving it a "lean-to" or, in modern architectural terms, "saltbox" appearance. It had a large twelve-foot center chimney, as well as five working fireplaces and a brick oven. Some of the features of the house include several "King's boards" (boards that had been cut to such a large width they were considered property of the king), shiplap sheathing of chestnut, hard pine floor, and handmade forged hinges and latches.

In 1701, the house ultimately became the property of a John Wood, and several generations of Woods lived in the house.

A significant and most interesting story about the occupants of the house lies within the Wood family archives. In 1757, Mary Wood, of the fourth generation, married Captain Samuel Allyn of Gales Ferry, who was a selectman of the town and a captain in the militia. As the story goes, in 1781, when the alarm was sounded that the British were about to attack Groton's Fort Griswold, Allyn got on his horse and went to the home of Ensign Amos Lester. Together they rode to the old

Wood house, where Allyn's sister Eunice, the wife of John Wood, lived. They left their horses at the house and walked the remaining distance to Fort Griswold. Allyn was slain during the battle, and Lester received a wound to his hip.

Unfortunately, little else has been documented concerning the occupants after the Wood families; however, ultimately, the "old red" house and property became the property of the Bailey family, who farmed the property connected to the house.

In the mid-1930s, the late Elmer D. Keith of North Haven, Connecticut, was employed by the Works Progress Administration to document every house in the state of Connecticut built before 1850. His research about the houses appears in a book titled *Connecticut: A Guide to Its Roads, Lore and People*. While conducting research in Groton, Keith came across the "old red house," now known as the Bailey tenant farmer house. The house had been vacant for almost a decade.

Keith, an eccentric historian antiquarian of sorts, had visions of constructing a historical village, similar to Massachusetts' Sturbridge Village. Feeling that the Groton house would make a fine addition to his vision and that it could also be used to house the caretaker of his farm in Clintonville, he reached an agreement with Burchard Bailey to purchase the house. He reportedly purchased the house for $75 and agreed to dismantle the house and have it moved from the site at no expense to Bailey.

The house was subsequently moved to and erected across from Keith house, the oldest stone house in Connecticut, on Clintonville Road in North Haven. Keith had also stored other dismantled buildings, including a milk house, in a barn on his property for use in his "village."

A search on the Internet revealed a listing for a house named "Old Gungywamp" at 892 Clintonville Road in Clintonville. A brief write-up stated: "circa 1670, it was originally located in Groton and moved to its present site in the 1920s by a local antiquarian."

In early October of last year, this writer and his wife traveled to North Haven in hopes of catching a glimpse of what might be remaining of the 330-year-old house. After some searching, the house was located and not only found to be in excellent condition but still occupied. To our surprise, the present owner, Sandra Weekes, was at home and graciously invited us in for a look. Ms. Weekes and her former husband purchased the house in late 1969 for $39,500. After a tour of the house, one must say, thanks to the many years of hard work and research by Ms. Weekes, it has maintained its original look and atmosphere. The house, which is now assessed at $385,000, is for sale, and I must say it would leave any historian in awe.

Sandra Weekes contributed to this article and provided this photograph picturing the "Old Gungywamp" house in Groton around 1900. *(January 10, 2008)*

The Old Gungywamp house circa 1900
(Courtesy Sandra Weekes)

# "Duffy"—Groton's U.S. Coast Guard Mascot

Man's best friends, dogs, have been serving their masters and all of mankind for many years. They are pets, friends, and companions. But more than this, they can be an integral part of a working team, as with seeing-eye dogs or law enforcement canines. For hundreds of years, military units have adopted animals as mascots, which, according to folklore, was thought to bring good luck.

I'm sure there have been hundreds, if not thousands, of visitors to the University of Connecticut's Avery Point campus in Groton who have observed the small grave headstone on the lawn overlooking Shennecossett and Eastern Point Beach and left wondering about its background. The face of the small granite headstone reads: "DUFFY BM 1/C USCG MASCOT," and the date "JAN 2, 47" is engraved on the top.

For those readers who may not be aware, during the period of 1942 through 1967, the Avery Point Campus was the home of the United States Coast Guard Training Station. Throughout the years, thousands of Coast Guardsmen were assigned to and received their training in a variety of schools at the Groton Station.

For over ten years, while actively involved in a project to restore the lighthouse at Avery Point, members of the Avery Point Lighthouse Society developed a keen interest in trying to find out the story about "DUFFY." Whenever contacts were made with men who had been stationed at the Station, questions were always asked, but, unfortunately, no one seemed to know anything about Duffy. Searches were made of the *Day* newspaper archives and various Coast Guard Training Station documents; again, to no avail.

The lighthouse society even placed an article in their lighthouse newsletter in the fall of 2004 requesting anyone having information to contact them. No responses were received, and it was thought that the story and history about Duffy would remain a mystery forever.

Then, in July of last year, out of an unexpected happenstance, this author and his wife met Alice Vross while having breakfast at a local restaurant. While talking with Mrs. Vross, she mentioned that her husband, Edward, had been stationed at the Coast Guard Station in the mid-1940s. Not being shy, I asked if she had any photographs of the Station, and she replied she did. Then, to my surprise, and shock, she mentioned she even had a photograph of Duffy and asked if I knew who he was. I immediately began to question her about Duffy, and she responded by saying that her husband knew all about [him], and that I should talk to him.

Within a few hours, my wife and I were sitting in the Vrosses' living room and being told the story about Duffy.

Duffy was described as being a stray mixed-breed bulldog, brown and white, with a large wart on his side and quite squat and fat. He had been adopted as the Station's mascot by the men prior to Vross arriving at the facility in 1944.

He was quartered with the fifteen to twenty security men at the Station's Guard House, which is now occupied by the UCONN campus police and, according to Vross, was treated like a king. As an example, each day a member of the security detachment would go to the mess hall and have a special plate fixed for Duffy. It was not unusual for his morning diet to include quite a few pieces of bacon and sausages. This certainly could account for his being squat and fat. Duffy was also fitted for and provided a special uniform so he could march with the guys during ceremonies at the Station. He also would accompany his caretakers while they walked their roving patrols.

Duffy was well behaved and was well accepted by everyone stationed at the base, including its commander.

Mr. Vross left Groton in 1946 and Duffy passed, for reasons unknown, a few months later.

Obviously Duffy was a loyal friend, comrade, and mascot to the men he served with at the Groton Coast Guard Station. He certainly earned the special resting place overlooking New London and Groton. It is nice to now know the mystery behind Duffy, and just as we say about other departed members—"you are not dead until you are forgotten." Duffy, you are not forgotten! *(January 3, 2008)*

Duffy's headstone at Avery Point
Note the flowers to the right of the marker, which an unknown
person replaces every year.
(Courtesy Jim Streeter)

# Before the Griswold Hotel

Although there have been numerous articles written about the elegant Griswold Hotel, many individuals are not aware that there were several other hotels that preceded the Griswold.

The Griswold Hotel was located in the part of Groton that, in the old days, was known as the "Eastern Point Colony." Albert Avery, who lived and began farming there in about 1837, owned most of the property on Eastern Point. By the early 1840s, Avery came up with the idea of transforming the property into a summer resort of sorts. At the time there were only two houses on Eastern Point, Avery's house and a hotel called the "Ocean House." This hotel was reportedly built in 1846 and operated by Captain Silas Fiske. It was a three-story wooden structure that resembled a farmhouse of sorts with two large additions. It was said to have had small rooms and narrow piazzas and corridors.

In 1873, a larger hotel, called the Edgecomb House, replaced the Ocean House. In 1884, the Sturtevant family of Norwich purchased this hotel, and, through costly improvements, doubled its size and renamed it the "Fort Griswold House." The new hotel was four stories high and had two separate two-story turret-tower structures on its roof. It had 175 rooms, all of which commanded a view of either the Thames River or Long Island Sound. Unlike its predecessor, the Fort Griswold House had a large and broad porch gallery traveling around the entire hotel for its guests to enjoy.

The hotel had three separate dining areas: a general dining area measuring thirty-five feet by ninety feet, a private dining room measuring fourteen feet by twenty-one feet, and a children's dining room measuring sixteen feet by thirty-six feet, the latter because it was not uncommon for vacationing parents to dine separately from their children.

The hotel boasted that, in the interest of hygiene, it was equipped with a waste piping system, which, with the help of gravity, carried the waste for discharge into the Thames River. Other amenities offered at this modern hotel included separate reading, smoking, and reception rooms, and parlors, as well as a children's playroom.

The Fort Griswold House
(Courtesy Jim Streeter)

In 1905, Morton Plant purchased the Fort Griswold House, and within a period of eight months, the hotel was razed and replaced with the larger and more modern Griswold Hotel.

All three of the hotels that preceded the Griswold Hotel were instrumental in promoting Eastern Point as one of the most popular areas in Connecticut for summer vacationing. *(April 12, 2007)*

# The Sister Hotel of Groton's Griswold Hotel

There have been many articles written about the former Griswold Hotel that was once located in the Eastern Point area of Groton. In its heyday, the Griswold was often described as the largest and most luxurious hotel on the Atlantic coast. For years it held its place among the most popular of the New England resort hotels, and it was not unusual for all of its four-hundred-plus rooms to be completely booked for the entire "summer season" running from June through September.

The Griswold Hotel was built in 1906 by Morton F. Plant, Groton's wealthy business tycoon, who inherited several railroad and steamship businesses amassed by his father, Henry B. Plant, in Florida. Henry Plant was responsible for developing railroad and steamship transportation networks that traveled from South Carolina and Georgia, through Jacksonville, and all along the west coast of Florida to Tampa.

In 1888, possibly out of a sense of competition with Henry Flagler, who was developing railroad routes on the east coast of Florida, along with several expensive hotels, Henry Plant decided to build his own grandiose hotel in Tampa. Completed in 1891 at a cost of about $3 million, Plant's Tampa Bay Hotel was indeed a masterpiece of ornate and fanciful design. It still stands today and is part of the University of Tampa.

Four years after building his Tampa Bay Hotel, Plant developed plans to build a luxury resort in a secluded site on a bluff overlooking Clearwater Bay near the Gulf of Mexico. The resort would include a planned community surrounding a hotel and would be more "relaxed and informal." It would offer various outdoor activities, including golf, bicycling, horseback riding, fishing, hunting, yachting, and tennis. There would be nightly performances by orchestras and bands. The name of the resort was the Belleview.

Construction of the resort began in the summer of 1895, and in January of 1897 the new four-story wooden Belleview Hotel, with its 145 rooms, opened. Advertisements for the hotel boast of each room having three lights, its own fireplace, polished floors, and oak and cherry furniture. Some of the amenities available in the hotel included telephone and telegraph services, a newsstand, and an in-house barber shop. The hotel was an immediate success.

After the unexpected death of Henry Plant in June of 1889, the operations of the hotel were assumed by Morton F. Plant. He subsequently added two large wings to the existing building, increasing the number of rooms to 425. He had the original wood exterior, which had faded to a dull brown, painted bright white, and then had the roof retiled with green shingles. The Belleview became known as the "White Queen of the Gulf." In 1915, he hired Donald J. Ross to design two golf courses at the resort. Interestingly, believing that the grasses for the golf greens would not grow in Florida, Plant had trainloads of topsoil shipped from Indiana to construct the greens.

The similarities between Plant's Belleview hotel and resort in Clearwater, Florida, and his Griswold Hotel in Groton are uncanny. Each hotel was four stories high, having four-hundred-plus rooms. They were both painted white and had green shingle roofs. Both facilities offered the same types of outdoor activities, including golf, swimming, tennis, yachting, and fishing. Morton Plant was certainly consistent in his development of his hotels.

Interestingly, many of the employees of the hotel became known as "snowbird workers," and, just as many residents do, they would travel between Connecticut and Florida during the off-seasons to remain working during the good weather months.

The Belleview has changed hands many times since the death of Morton Plant in 1918; however, it is still in operation today as the Belleview Biltmore Resort. A few years ago, my wife and I made a special trip to Clearwater and spent three days at the hotel. Having been familiar with the Griswold Hotel, and while touring the older portions of the Belleview, I can only describe the experience as a bit of déjà vu. The Belleview and the Griswold Hotels, in my opinion, were indeed sister hotels.

Those readers who remember the Griswold, or those who never visited but would like to know what that hotel was like, should pay a visit to the Belleview. You'd be amazed! *(May 22, 2008)*

# Morton F. Plant's Three Farms

In the late 1890s, millionaire Morton F. Plant decided to build his summer resort in Groton. There was a great deal of speculation as to why Plant, whose wealth ranked right up there with the Rockefellers, Asters, and Vanderbilts, selected Groton rather than the fashionable and wealthy Newport to build his great estate. It has been said that Plant had a great interest and desire to be a gentleman farmer, and it was the availability of a vast amount of undeveloped land on which to build his dream farms that led him to Groton.

Initially, Plant purchased approximately seventy acres of property at Avery Point in the Eastern Point section of the town, on which he built the Branford House, his thirty-one-room mansion. A large, modern, heated greenhouse and several outdoor nurseries along with cold-frame gardens were also built and took up a considerable amount of the estate's property. Many of the flowers grown on the estate, specifically the orchids, carnations, chrysanthemums, and roses, won prizes at flower shows throughout the country. Also grown in Plant's greenhouse were various tropical plants and flowers, including the famous "Venus flytraps." It was said that many mice on the property were consumed by these "meat-eating" plants. Vegetable gardens provided a variety of vegetables for Morton Plant, his visitors, and the staff of fifty that took care of the facilities.

In the early 1900s, Plant began to actively pursue his desire and dream of becoming a farmer. He purchased hundreds of acres of farmlands in Groton to build his produce, poultry, livestock, and dairy farms. These farms would ultimately become known as Branford Farms.

Plant developed his poultry business on the former Mather farm, where the Branford Avenue apartment complex is located today. It was equipped with the most modern of equipment, including electric lights and automatic feed hoppers in all of it coops and pens. The farm boasted housing over ten thousand egg-laying hens and having the ability to supply and deliver fresh eggs on a daily basis throughout New London County. The Branford Poultry Farm also sold broiler chickens and native turkeys, which were raised on the farm.

In 1911, after acquiring the 250-acre Morgan Farm, on the property now occupied by the Groton–New London Airport, Plant built one of the largest and most productive dairy farms in southeastern Connecticut. The barns, considered to be the most modern at the time, were constructed of cement and finished on the exterior in stucco. The interior floors were cement, and there were metal stanchions throughout. All of Plant's barns, unlike others in the state, were equipped with electricity, running water (both hot and cold), and steam heat. The Branford Dairy Farm had over three hundred head of Guernsey and Ayrshire cows, and it was said that Plant's cattle were the best known—and the most pampered—in New England.

Several veterinarians were employed to keep the cows under close observation to ensure a healthy herd. Before milking, each cow was carefully groomed and thoroughly washed; the milking equipment was sterilized to provide the highest quality milk. There were bottling and cooling facilities on the farm. The farm produced not only milk but fresh cream, butter, buttermilk, koumiss, and cream cheese. A variety of vegetables were also grown on the farm.

The cattle farm produced many prize-winning cows and bulls, and several of Plant's award-winning Guernseys sold, at average, for almost $2,400 each at public auction.

Not too well-known is the fact that Plant established a third farm in the area. In the early 1900s, he purchased an estimated three thousand acres of land in East Lyme, a portion of which is used today by the Connecticut National Guard for training. Ultimately, Plant converted the property into a private game preserve where he and his friends could hunt and fish. Named the Plantford Farm, it was well equipped for raising various game birds, including prized English ring-necked pheasants and Hungarian partridges, quail, ruffled grouse, woodcocks, wild turkeys, and various breeds of ducks. A small part of the farm was also used to breed and raise pedigree pigs and sheep.

Most of the eggs, milk, meats, poultry, produce, and vegetables served at Plant's famous Griswold Hotel Resort in Groton were supplied by these three farms.

After the death of Plant in 1918, the federal government filed a court claim seeking to recover a large amount of unpaid income tax from his estate for the profits they felt he realized from the farms. Although on the surface it appeared that the farms were extremely profitable, it was argued that Plant was not engaged in farming as a business but more for pleasure. It was also shown that the farms were operating at a tremendous loss.

In 1914, Plant provided the Connecticut Fish and Game Commission with a ten-year lease to the Plantford Farm in East Lyme. Some years later, much of the property was divided into various-size plots and sold outright.

The Branford Farms continued to operate in Groton for some years after the death of Plant. The farm property used to raise his cattle was subsequently acquired by the State of Connecticut for use as an airport, and the poultry farm property was acquired for the federal government to build housing at the beginning of World War II. *(September 25, 2008)*

# Eastern Point Stagecoach

Recently I acquired a photograph showing a stagecoach in front of a livery stable in Mystic. A description written on the back of the photo indicated that the stagecoach made trips from Newport, Rhode Island, and Eastern Point in Groton.

Subsequent research revealed the stable to be the Bank Square Livery and Boarding Stables, which was on Water Street (today's Bank Square) in Mystic. Roswell Brown started the business in the early 1850s. In 1883, his son, James E. F. Brown, joined the business. The stable had twenty-four stalls and boasted of having the most comfortable and stylish coaches available. Horses provided by the livery were considered to be in the finest of physical condition, well groomed, and to have very reliable dispositions.

In the early days of the business, Roswell Brown operated a stagecoach route from Mystic to Stonington for passengers who would be taking boats to New York from the latter. The livery also provided carriage service to and from the Mystic railroad station.

Curious about the information written on the back of the photograph, I asked my dear friend Carol Kimball, who is also Groton's knowledgeable historian, about stagecoach runs from Newport to Eastern Point. She immediately stated that, to her knowledge, there had been only one such excursion and it was made by Charles O. Williams, Jr.'s, specially built stagecoach "Tantivy." The trip took place around the turn of the century. Interestingly, Mr. Williams was an avid horseman who owned dozens of fine horses. He was the president of the Groton Driving Association in Poquonnock Bridge, and many of his horses won races on the oval horse track of Groton Driving Park across from the present Poquonnock Plains Park.

The "Tantivy" made about fifteen trips from Stonington to Groton's Fort Griswold House, the predecessor of the Griswold Hotel. The trips would take a little over two hours to complete, having three stops— one in Mystic, one at the top of Fort Hill, and one in Poquonnock—to change and rest the team of horses. The stop and change of horses in Mystic was made at the Bank Square Livery.

A few weeks ago, I wrote an article about the development of the large operate the business. The Albertus B. Brown automobile storage and Wally's Service Station later occupied the livery property. *(April 26, 2007)*

# Midway Train Wrecks

A few weeks ago I wrote an article about the development of the large Midway railroad yard and facilities in Poquonnock Bridge. The article relayed that, at its peak, the yard would handle between thirty-five and forty freight trains daily, and it was not uncommon to have trains of over half a mile in length lined up on spare tracks west and east of the facility.

Along with the increase in railroad traffic at Midway came incidents involving train accidents. Unfortunately, two of the accidents, one in May of 1912 and the second in July of 1917, tragically resulted in the death of two individuals.

One of the most spectacular train wrecks in the area happened on the early morning of December 21, 1924, when an eastbound Pittsburgh express train crashed into a seventy-two-car freight train that was crossing the trunk line at Midway. The express train was comprised of a locomotive and ten cars. Some of the freight cars were carrying rough-cut granite tombstones and were derailed when the locomotive of the express struck the train. The express train was traveling at approximately 40 miles per hour when the crash occurred.

The impact of the crash caused the derailment of eight freight cars and threw many of the two hundred passengers on the express from their berths in sleeping cars and from seats in the coach cars. Fortunately, no one was killed, and only eight individuals sustained minor injuries as a result of the accident. Miraculously, the engineer and firemen in the locomotive of the express train escaped without injury.

Train traffic traveling through the area was disrupted for hours while wrecking crews and two special wrecking trains from Midway cleared the tracks of debris. After several hours of cleaning up, only one of the four track lines was opened for through traffic. Approximately 150 feet of track and roadbed were damaged during the accident, and the estimated repair cost was set at approximately $20,000.

A probe into the cause of the accident revealed that the express train had been delayed at various locations along its route to its final destination of Boston and was about one and a half hours behind schedule just prior to the accident occurring. The train's crew, while attempting to make up the lost time, ran a "cautionary signal" and subsequently ran onto a track over which the freight was passing. *(February 1, 2007)*

# Groton's Trolleys

Back in the early 1900s and continuing until the late 1920s, one of the major modes of transportation in Groton was the trolley.

The Groton and Stonington Street Railway Company was organized in August of 1903, and trolleys began running in December of 1904. Trolleys ran back and forth from Groton to Westerly, Rhode Island, hourly, with the first leaving Groton at 6:20 AM and the last arriving in Westerly at 11:45 PM. The trolleys made frequent stops at various locations in the business districts of Mystic and Groton. The trip between Groton and Westerly would take approximately one hour and twenty-five minutes and cost five cents.

The company built several waiting rooms so passengers could protect themselves from bad weather. One such waiting room was located at the entrance to Groton Long Point.

The end of the line for trolleys arriving in Groton was at the intersection of Thames and School streets. The motorman on the trolley would manually turn the vehicle around on tracks at that intersection so it could begin its travel to Westerly.

In the late 1920s, an increase in motor vehicle use on the same streets on which the trolley traveled caused a considerable amount of traffic congestion. Buses rapidly began to take the place of the trolleys, and in July of 1928 the use of trolleys in Groton was discontinued. *(March 21, 2006)*

Trolley turnaround on Thames Street
(Courtesy Jim Streeter)

# Groton's Toll Bridges

Some readers believe that recent suggestions of charging tolls on highways and bridges in Connecticut would be a new and creative way of raising revenues for the highways; however, to many Groton residents this idea is "old hat."

Prior to 1919, the only way for motor vehicles to cross the Thames River was by ferry. A fee, or toll of sorts, was charged for this service.

In October 1919, the New Haven Railroad opened a new railroad bridge across the river to replace one built in 1889. The State of Connecticut, after receiving numerous complaints about the inadequacy of the ferry in handling increased amounts of traffic, subsequently purchased the old railroad bridge and converted it into a motor vehicle bridge. The State provided the Town of Groton and the City of New London the options of either having a toll bridge (owned by the state) or a "free bridge," which would cost Groton $80,000 and New London $120,000 to help defray the costs of converting the bridge. In the interest of saving the "up-front" money, both communities decided on the toll bridge. The tolls charged were certainly not cheap by today's standards—thirty cents for two-seated automobiles, plus five cents for each additional passenger; five cents for pedestrians; and anywhere from twenty cents to thirty-five cents for horse-drawn vehicles. The toll bridge subsequently proved to be a "gold mine" for the State. The convenience of the bridge resulted in toll receipts increasing in leaps and bounds, and within six months the average monthly take from the tolls was close to $10,000.

In 1923, the Connecticut General Assembly, after a four-year battle, voted to cease collecting tolls on all Connecticut bridges, including the Thames River Bridge, as of December 31st of that year.

Although the converted railroad bridge was more convenient and quicker than the ferryboat system, it did have a few drawbacks. The travel portion of the bridge was extremely narrow, and it was often necessary to stop traffic in one direction to permit large vehicles or wide loads to cross in the opposite direction. The bridge was also a swing bridge and traffic was frequently stopped in both directions to open the bridge for boat traffic on the river.

Beginning as early as 1927, efforts were under way to replace the bridge with a newer high-level span. Approval to construct the bridge was given by the General Assembly in 1939; however, funding for its construction was curtailed. By the early 1940s, with the large expansion of the Electric Boat Company in Groton, the increase in traffic over the bridge resulted in lengthy bottlenecks, which brought the need for a new bridge to a head. In short order, funding in the amount of $6,000,000 for the new bridge and $2,000,000 for improvements of the highways leading to the bridge was approved. There were two stipulations contained in the legislative bill granting the money. The first required that the State be reimbursed for the money used to build the bridge through the collection of tolls, and the second mandated that the old bridge be immediately demolished upon completion of the construction of the new bridge.

Actual construction of the new cantilever-truss-deck bridge began in February of 1941 and the new Groton–New London Bridge was open to traffic on February 27, 1943. The bridge, which was a little over 1.1 miles in length, boasted of having the longest cantilever span in New England. With a clearance height of 135 feet, it was the highest bridge in Connecticut and was considered high enough to permit the passage of the largest vessels ever likely to navigate the river. Its roadway was forty-eight feet wide, which permitted four vehicular lanes of traffic—two south and two north.

Toll collection booths and an administration building were erected on the Groton side of the bridge. The original toll charged was fifteen cents for a single (one-way) trip of passenger automobiles and horse-drawn vehicles, sixty cents for tractor-trailer trucks and buses, and two cents for pedestrians. Books containing one hundred tickets for passenger vehicles, which could be purchased for $3, drastically reduced toll costs for those who made frequent trips over the bridge. Over the years, there were several reductions in the tolls charged. Ultimately, the toll for an automobile was ten cents, and pedestrians crossed free of charge.

As a point of interest, in 1951 the name of the bridge was changed to the Gold Star Memorial Bridge to honor those who had lost their lives in World Wars I and II.

In March of 1963, the collecting of tolls was discontinued on the bridge. The primary reason for removing the tolls was to make the bridge and its connecting roads eligible for federal highway grants. The federal government would not contribute toward projects where tolls were charged.

By the early 1960s, after the Interstate 95 highway system connected to the bridge, and with dramatic increases in employment levels at the Electric Boat and Pfizer companies, the four-lane Gold Star Bridge soon became inadequate to handle the amount of traffic associated with these changes.

Beginning in the late 1960s, a new six-lane truss-deck bridge was constructed next to the Gold Star Bridge. Upon completion of that bridge, the Gold Star was refitted into a six-lane bridge. Today traffic traveling through Groton and New London over these twin six-lane "toll-free" bridges runs very smoothly. *(August 7, 2008)*

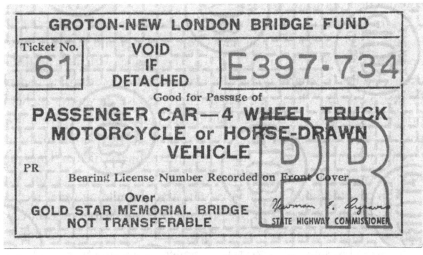

A Gold Star Memorial Bridge toll ticket
(Courtesy Jim Streeter)

# North Pole Expeditions by Two Nautilus Submarines

Recently I read that a resolution was introduced in the United States Congress by Connecticut Representative Joe Courtney recognizing the upcoming fiftieth anniversary of the USS *Nautilus* (*SSN 571*) voyage to the North Pole under the Arctic ice cap. Indeed, it was a great achievement that led to many other expeditions for scientific research and exploration.

In his introduction of the resolution, Representative Courtney also mentioned that the *Nautilus* was the first submarine to journey "20,000 leagues under the sea." This statement was a tongue-in-cheek remark relating to the Jules Verne novel *Twenty Thousand Leagues Under the Sea* in 1870 that detailed the exploits of a make-believe submarine named *Nautilus*.

I am sure that few readers are aware that in June of 1931, some twenty-seven years earlier, another American submarine, also named the *Nautilus*, attempted to make the same historic journey under the Arctic.

In the late 1920s, Sir Hubert Wilkins, the famous Australian photographer and explorer, teamed up with American explorer Lincoln Ellsworth to conduct an Arctic expedition that included reaching the North Pole under the ice. In early 1931, they purchased the decommissioned World War I submarine USS *O-12* (*SS73*) from the United States Navy for the sum of one dollar. The submarine, which had been built by the Lake Torpedo Boat Company in Bridgeport, Connecticut, was subsequently renamed the *Nautilus* and was modified for the proposed under-ice mission. Of interest was the fact that Jean Jules Verne, the grandson of novelist Jules Verne, traveled from France to be present when the new *Nautilus* was christened. In deference to the laws at the time banning alcohol, a small silver barrel containing cracked ice was used to christen the ship. It was also said that the use of the ice was symbolic because the ship was to cross the top of the world under ice.

Old Lyme resident Sloan Danenhower, a civilian and former submarine commander, was selected to captain the *Nautilus*. He hand-selected each of the twenty crew members to make the trip under the Arctic.

Before setting out on the expedition, the *Nautilus* was put through several test runs in various locations off the New England coast, including Block Island. During this period of time, it was home ported at the New London Submarine Base in Groton. A few days before leaving the Sub Base, the crew loaded their food rations for the trip. These included thirteen hundred pounds of butter, twelve hundred pounds of evaporated milk, seven hundred pounds of coffee, forty-four hundred pounds of sugar, twenty-six hundred pounds of flour, three thousand pounds of meat and fish, and numerous cases of canned fruit and vegetables, sauces, baked beans, powdered eggs, and milk.

In June 1931 the *Nautilus* departed on its polar journey. In late August the submarine experienced major mechanical failures and sustained massive hull damage and engine failure after encountering a storm, and the *Nautilus* was forced to cancel the expedition. They had not successfully crossed the North Pole under the ice.

Following the expedition, the *Nautilus* was returned to the Navy Department and was scuttled in November of 1931. Thus is the story of the short but interesting life of the first submarine named *Nautilus*.

As an addendum to this story, in 1959 the nuclear submarine USS *Skate* was the second submarine to reach the North Pole, and while there the ship's crew conducted a tribute ceremony to Sir George Hubert Wilkins and scattered his ashes over the North Pole. *(April 24, 2008)*

The *Nautilus*, March 31, 1931
*Left to right*, Sloan Danenhower, commander of the boat; Jean Jules
Verne, grandson of author Jules Verne; and Sir Hubert Wilkins
(Courtesy Jim Streeter)

# Groton's "Fairview"—The Odd Fellows Home of Connecticut

A few weeks ago, I was asked about the large stone building that overlooks the Thames River from a hill on the west side of the Military Highway leading to the Submarine Base. The person who was asking thought it was some type of private school.

I explained that the building was called "Fairview," or the "Odd Fellows Home," and that it was a nonprofit elder care and independent living facility. Of course, the words "Odd Fellows" produced further inquiry about the inhabitants of Fairview. Any possible suspicions about the residents being strange or out of the ordinary were quickly dispelled after I provided some background about the highly respected fraternal organization called the Independent Order of Odd Fellows that established the "Home."

The history of the Fairview and the Odd Fellows Home is quite interesting.

In 1833, Belton A. Copp, who had previously been postmaster in St. Mary's, Georgia, moved to Groton. In 1837, he purchased a two-hundred-acre farm on the banks of the Thames River from Latham Avery. The present Odd Fellows Home property is located in the southwest corner of the original farm.

In the early 1840s, Colonel Robert Stafford, an extremely rich southern cotton farmer, began spending his summers in Groton with Mr. Copp. Stafford had six children whom he sent north to be educated. In 1853, he decided to build a home in Groton where he could spend his summers with his family. He subsequently purchased thirty-three acres of the Copp farm, on which he had a Southern-style mansion built for $25,000. The house had nineteen rooms, and a cottage annex had six additional rooms. Also built at the same time were a barn, a carriage house, and an ice house. In 1886, Stafford purchased an additional twelve acres of land from Copp.

Up until the beginning of the Civil War, Stafford spent several weeks every summer at his mansion. When the Civil War began, he returned South and never came back to Groton. His daughter Mary continued to live in the house with her husband, Charles Gaylord, MD, and their son. Mary died in 1879, and in 1886 the house was sold to Mary A. Hoadley, who reportedly named the property "Fairview" for the magnificent river views it provided. Hoadley subsequently married William Flemming, and in 1892 the Fairview property was sold to the Connecticut Grand Lodge of the International Order of Odd Fellows for $13,000.

The Odd Fellows Fairview Home was officially dedicated in April of 1883. Throughout the years, many additions and improvements have been made at Fairview. A thirty-one-room wooden dormitory was added in 1904, and in 1926 a fifty-room granite infirmary was built to offer complete medical services. An auditorium was constructed in 1959, and a 120-bed nursing home wing was added in 1978. In 2007, a sixteen-thousand-square-foot addition to the nursing-care facility was added.

The beginning of International Order of Odd Fellows (IOOF) can be traced back to about the second quarter of the eighteenth century, when a "secret fraternal, benefit society" was founded in England. A Grand Lodge of the organization formed in London in 1803. The first official American lodge is believed to have been established in Baltimore, Maryland, in 1819. The Connecticut Lodge was established in 1840.

Initially, the principal mission of the Connecticut Odd Fellows Home was to care for the aged and indigent Odd Fellows, their wives, and orphans. The principals practiced by IOOF members are friendship, love, and truth.

Although the true reason for the name "Odd Fellows" is not known, an interesting and plausible explanation provided by many members of the organization is the fact that "when common laborers originally associated themselves together and formed a fraternity for social unity, fellowship and for mutual help, it was against all trends of the times [England 1700]. Thus they became known as 'peculiar' or 'odd' and subsequently derived the name 'Odd Fellows.'"

Today Groton's Odd Fellows Home is considered one of the most advanced and comprehensive elder-care facilities in Connecticut. No longer is membership in the International Order of Odd Fellows required for admission—it is open to the public who are over the age of fifty-five. Not only has Fairview remained true to its original purpose, but it has also grown to include what is called "Fellowship Manor," an independent-living retirement community.

Groton can be proud of the facilities and services provided at Fairview. Our citizens owe a debt of gratitude to the Connecticut Lodge of Odd Fellows for selecting our community for their "Home" and for the continued support they provide to this wonderful facility. *(December 11, 2008)*

# The Resolute Desk

The next time you watch the president of the United States deliver a speech from the Oval Office of the White House, take a close look at the desk he is sitting at—it has a Groton connection.

In 1855, Captain James Monroe Buddington of Center Groton went on a whaling expedition to the Arctic. In September of that year, while traveling through the ice fields in Davis Strait, located between Greenland and the Baffin Island in the Canadian territory of Nunavut, Buddington and his crew observed an abandoned ship in the ice. The ship was the British vessel HMS *Resolute*, which had been on a mission to find the missing British explorer Sir John Franklin. The boat had been stuck in the ice and abandoned for a period of over six months.

Because whaling in the area was not as plentiful as on previous trips, Buddington believed it would be more profitable to salvage the vessel rather than continue the whaling expedition. Buddington and his crew freed the boat and brought it back to New London.

Buddington subsequently sold the vessel to the U.S. Government for the handsome price of $40,000. It was refitted and restored and presented to Queen Victoria as an expression of friendship between the two nations.

Three years after being rescued, the HMS *Resolute* returned to service and served for twenty-one years before being decommissioned. In 1879, after the vessel was taken out of service, Queen Victoria ordered that three desks be made from the timbers of the ship. One was presented to the wife of the man who had financed the trip to find Sir John Franklin; the second was given to Captain Buddington; and the third was delivered to the White House as a token of appreciation from the Queen. President Rutherford B. Hayes accepted the desk, which has been used by every president since.

The original desk did not have a front panel. In 1944, President Franklin D. Roosevelt ordered that a hinged panel, carved with the presidential seal, be installed to hide his leg braces and wheelchair. The panel was not installed until after his death in 1945.

One memory of the desk is the famous photograph of President John F. Kennedy sitting there while his son plays beneath.

Incidentally, the whereabouts of the desk presented to Groton's Captain Buddington is unknown. *(December 7, 2006)*

The Resolute Desk
(Courtesy Carol Kimball)

# About the Author

James L. ("Jim") Streeter is a lifelong resident of the town of Groton. He recently retired as a forensic science examiner for the State of Connecticut. His interest in Groton's history began while he was employed as a police officer in the City of Groton in the late 1960s.

Jim's involvement in the local community is diverse and extensive. He serves on the Board of Trustees for the Bill Memorial Library, the New London Maritime Society, and the Avery-Copp Museum, and is president of the Groton Historical Society. He is also very active in the saving and restoration of America's lighthouses by serving as the cofounder and cochairman of the Avery Point Lighthouse Society, vice president of the American Lighthouse Foundation, and vice president of the New London Ledge Lighthouse Foundation.

He has written a weekly historical article about Groton for the *Groton Times* newspaper since September of 2004 and has coauthored two *Images of America* books about Groton.